The Centennial Collection
More of Emily Ruete, born Sayyida Salme,
Princess of Oman and Zanzibar

By Andrea Emily Stumpf

Copyright © 2024 Andrea E. Stumpf
First edition; published in the United States, 2024
Cover design: Andrea E. Stumpf
Copy Editor: Lauri Scherer, LSF Editorial
Graphic Designer: Joe Bernier, Bernier Graphics

Huge appreciation to my book publishing team, Lauri, Bob, and Joe. Let it be said: There is no better partner on graphic design than Joe Bernier. Thank you!

Andrea E. Stumpf has asserted her right as copyright owner of this publication, including under the Copyright, Designs and Patents Act of 1988, to be identified as the author of this work, including as translator of the translated texts contained herein.

The original texts that were translated for *The Centennial Collection* come from handwritten documents from Emily Ruete, born Sayyida Salme, Princess of Oman and Zanzibar, and her children. They were subsequently typed and included as part of her *Literarischer Nachlass* (literary estate) that was granted to the Oriental Institute in Leiden in 1937, along with a number of other collected materials. This special collection was moved as a permanent loan to the Netherlands Institute for the Near East (NINO) in 1977 and became part of the Leiden University Libraries in 2018 as the Said-Ruete Archive, Or. 27.135.

All rights reserved. No part of this book may be reproduced, translated, or transmitted in any form or by any means, electronic or hard copy, including by photocopying, recording, any storage or retrieval system, or otherwise, without prior written permission of the author, translator, and copyright owner. For permission, send a request with complete information to andrea@sayyidasalme.com.

www.sayyidasalme.com; www.emilyruete.com

ISBN 978-1-7323975-7-6

Lest we forget those who slaved and served,

this book is dedicated to

Djilfidan.

1924–2024

To commemorate the centennial anniversary of Sayyida Salme's death in 1924, this book is presented in 2024 as a collection of writings and images that complement two previously published companion books. It is the third in a series after:

Memoirs of an Arabian Princess:
An Accurate Translation of Her Authentic Voice (2022)

Letters to the Homeland:
An Accurate Translation of an Intimate Voice (2023)

All references to the *Memoirs* and *Letters* that appear in footnotes and elsewhere in this *Centennial Collection* are to these books. All three books also appear as a combined set in *The Centennial Compilation: All of Emily Ruete, born Sayyida Salme, Princess of Oman and Zanzibar* (2024).

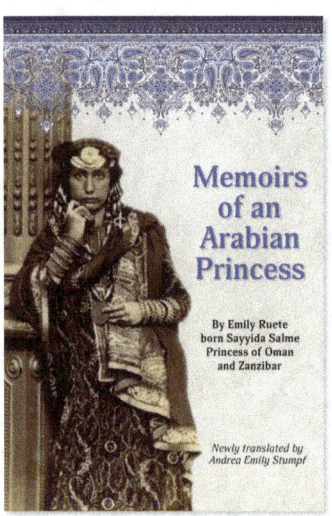
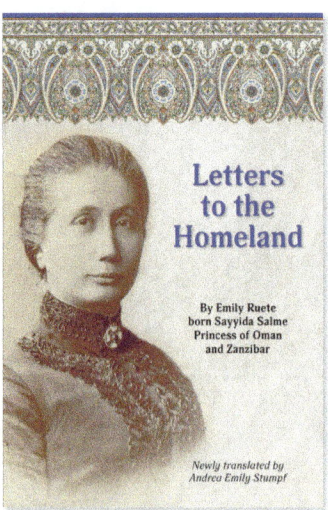
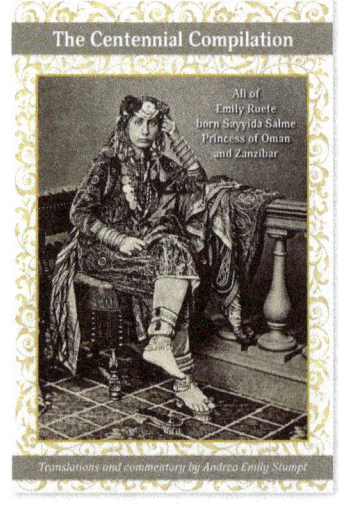

CONTENTS

Introduction	On Transits 6

Translations	**Addendum to My Memoirs** About the Addendum .... 12 Addendum to My Memoirs .... 22 **Syrian Customs and Conventions** About Syrian Customs and Conventions .... 36 Syrian Customs and Conventions 46

Remembrance	On Faith .... 54 On Legacy .... 76 In Memoriam .... 80 Salam 108

List of Images 109

ON TRANSITS

Being "trans" has a specific meaning nowadays, but it is a condition we have all felt to some degree or another. Some of us have had relatively simple lives with fewer transits. Many of us, however—more than in Sayyida Salme's time, and more and more as the world changes and the ground keeps shifting—have journeyed across borders and boundaries, and transcended limits, both in the wider world and in our own minds. Often, change comes to us, both subtle and seismic. The question then is what we make of the change, how we choose to respond when things happen beyond our control. But whether we are responding to change or making our own, it is a good thing to have room to move and maneuver. It is essential to our self-preservation and self-expression that each of us, in our own way, can create and claim our own space, to reach for better, more authentic, more fitting and fulfilling lives. It is a good thing when we have choice.

Sayyida Salme had all the instinct to reach, but only minimal room to choose. Living a hemmed-in life was perhaps typical for her time, and it was certainly part of her place in society. As a Muslim, a woman, a princess, each identity drew an ever tighter concentric circle around her being. I just want to breathe, she might have said at some point. And then she opened a window, which became a door, and then a vista beyond anything she had ever known.

Sometimes we step off the ledge into the unknown, trusting in ourselves, in God, or simply finding ourselves compelled to move forward. Have you been there? And once we have tasted the fruit, or learned what we did not know, then what has transpired cannot be undone. In Sayyida Salme's day, so many forces conspired to keep her in a narrow lane, and once she transgressed, those same forces closed ranks to deny her return.

Transgressed. Society lets us know when we have transgressed. We do not need a scarlet A to be shunned, and we are perhaps more likely to conform than clash anyhow. I admire those who raise the stakes to be themselves. As we see with Sayyida Salme and so many others, it is not easy. It has consequences. It can cut to the core. A single transgressive choice can cast a shadow for life. And if transgressive enough, it can trigger so much more lack of choice. Sayyida Salme took a step out of the box that became a slippery slope that moved across oceans and hemispheres, cultures and civilizations. She kept transiting as the bridges crashed in behind her. And she kept persisting, as she transformed into something much bigger than her transgression.

On Transits

Sayyida Salme escaped on the British Highflyer *in 1866*

Transformed. Her shortest chapter in the *Memoirs* is called "Great Transformations"[1]—that is the translation I chose for her German *Grosse Wandlungen*—while the *Letters* then fill in the details. Her transition that started with love was more than mere change; it was a total reverberation, a metamorphosis, an unmasking and unspooling into a new self. And it did not happen in an instant. It drew definition over time, as she kept defining her own world, transcribing her own thoughts, and making her own mark. All the while, she grounded herself in her beliefs and values and sense of self. This, I believe, is how she steadied herself over all the challenging terrain that she traversed.

Translated. I have had the great privilege of transiting Sayyida Salme's words from her original German into our modern lingua franca. I have also had the audacity to make that choice, to allow myself to substitute my words for hers, even as I have tried (together with my dear mother) to be as accurate and authentically true to her as possible. But playing with words is just one way to translate; we translate our experience into perspectives and choices every day. We translate ourselves to others, so they might better understand us, and they reflect those translations back to us, so we might better understand them.

---

[1] Her other very short chapter is about another transition, the move with her mother to Bet il Tani. This was the last of three childhood moves, having come from Bet il Mtoni, where she was born, and then moving to Bet il Watoro, where her mother—still a slave—supported her half-brother Madjid's family. Sayyida Salme moved thrice more before leaving Zanzibar, first to her plantation Kizimbani, then to Bububu on the coast, and finally to that fateful home in Stone Town. In that last move, she did as then-Sultan Madjid asked, even though she knew the city spelled trouble: "I had a dark premonition that new and inevitable misunderstandings awaited me there." (*Memoirs*, p. 194) These many relocations on the island previewed her many moves in Germany—five towns in ten years, each time to elude poverty, and then two more after she returned from Beirut at age 70. See the map of Germany in the *Letters* (p. 121; also footnote 199, p. 131).

To be sure, words often fail. And there is much that Sayyida Salme did not write. We cannot be fully transparent even to ourselves. What we say, what we convey—and how others translate that into their understanding—is never really straightforward. But we can still be grateful for the incredible range and depth of detail that Sayyida Salme left us of a time and place that would otherwise have disappeared from view. Now we are left to translate that into the world today, to find the relevance that shows us how history rhymes and teaches us about ourselves. I hope my translations of her writings[2] will enable many others to learn more about the past, reflect on the present, and take inspiration for the future.

———•———

I will bring this opening essay to a close with the very last words Sayyida Salme published in her own name—her last sentence at the end of the "Afterword" to her *Memoirs*, a text that was originally written in English as an addition to the official 1888 English translation:

> *My task is done—and, in conclusion, it only remains for me to say farewell to my kind readers, who have followed me through these pages, and who, I trust, will always bear a friendly memory for one whose life has already gathered so rich a store of changes and vicissitudes.* (Memoirs, p. 229)

Changes and vicissitudes. Thus ending the English version of her *Memoirs*, she gave us an apt, if understated, summation of what her life had been to date. We can put the emphasis on *vicissitudes*—a word that sounds like slithering sand sucked into time—to capture not just the mutability of it all, but also our exposure and vulnerability to external forces as we are whisked through our lives.

> vicissitude • \vuh-SISS-uh-tood\ • noun. 1: the quality or state of being changeable: mutability; 2a: a favorable or unfavorable event or situation that occurs by chance: a fluctuation of state or condition; 2b: a difficulty or hardship usually beyond one's control. Example: "The vicissitudes of life strike us all."[3]

---

2   All of these translations have been combined in a separate book, *The Centennial Compilation: Writings from Emily Ruete, born Sayyida Salme, Princess of Oman and Zanzibar* (2024), which bundles the three companion books: the *Memoirs* (2022), the *Letters* (2023), and this *Centennial Collection* (2024).
3   From the online Merriam-Webster Word of the Day for November 28, 2016.

On Transits

Sayyida Salme certainly felt the vicissitudes of life. We can read and feel that in what she left us. Those writings are, for now, enduring markers in the sand, as they harken back to an almost unimaginable past—taking us from her fantastical childhood to a drastic turning point to the tragic and transformative sequel. She gave us the bright and dark, the mundane and undaunted. These writings not only entertain, but also enlighten. Indeed, the latter was her mission, to "contribute my share . . . in removing many misconceptions and distortions." (*Memoirs*, p. 229) Her task is now mine in a new time and place, as I help transport[4] her words about the many changes and vicissitudes across languages and generations.

Many of the borders and boundaries that shaped Sayyida Salme's struggles are not the barriers they once were. Not to be taken for granted, we have more range to choose our transits and chart our transitions today. And yet, her bold and steadfast way may still speak to us. Even as the world gives us never-ending changes and vicissitudes, Sayyida Salme shows us what it means to believe in our own choices.

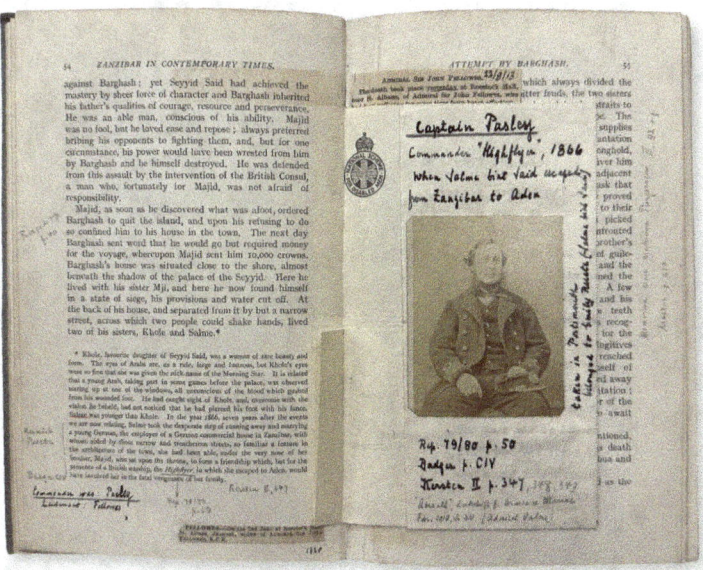

Captain Thomas Pasley took Sayyida Salme from Zanzibar to Aden

---

4   That totals ten trans words. Did you catch them all?

Literarischer Nachlass

von

EMILY RUETE

(Seyyidah Salme bint Said bin Sultan)

geb. 30. August 1844 in Zansibar,

gest. 29. Februar 1924 in Jena.

In Ergänzung

der

"Memoiren einer Arabischen Prinzessin."

Berlin 1886.

Translated:

Literary Estate of *EMILY RUETE* (Seyyidah Salme bint Said bin Sultan), born August 30, 1844, in Zanzibar, died February 29, 1924, in Jena.

As a supplement to the "Memoirs of an Arabian Princess," Berlin 1886.

ABOUT THE ADDENDUM

After twenty years in Germany, Sayyida Salme returned to Zanzibar in 1885 with excitement and hope, but left disappointed. She returned three years later in 1888, hopeful again, but ended up disappointed again—and jaded and bitter. For all the joy in seeing her homeland, and all the love and acceptance she was shown by the people, she failed to reconcile with her Sultan siblings, Sayyid Barghash on the first trip and Sayyid Chalife on the second.[5] That also meant she failed to secure any of the inheritance she believed she was entitled to. As she repeatedly stated, her pursuit of these claims was tied to the well-being of her children, for them more than for herself. Her impoverished circumstances animated her quest in a way that would not have been necessary had her husband survived.

With her conversion to Christianity, becoming an apostate seemed an obvious disqualifier for any claims to the family estate. Sayyida Salme, however, persisted over the decades in wide-ranging efforts to obtain her fractional portion from, as she

Sultan Chalife (1888–1890)

calculated in 1888, the twenty-one siblings who had since died.[6] She had already received her full portion of the father's estate outright at the unusually young age of 12. This consisted primarily of a large sum of money and several plantations and was expected to support both her and her mother.[7] Once in Germany, she had also been sent a gift by her late brother, Sayyid Madjid, although it mysteriously never reached her.[8] But Sayyid Barghash was not to be swayed; he showed not one iota of empathy or filial attachment. To the contrary, her repeated efforts, including through direct correspondence, and any sporadic German and British diplomatic inquiries, seemed only to irritate his already irascible stance. Sadly, whatever relief and excitement Sayyida Salme felt when Sayyid Chalife took the mantle also became a painful exercise in futility and humiliation.

---

5 Sayyid Barghash bin Said reigned from 1870 to 1888; Sayyid Chalife (Khalifa) bin Said from 1888 to 1890.
6 E. van Donzel, *An Arabian Princess Between Two Worlds: Memoirs, Letters, Sequels to the Memoirs, Syrian Customs and Usages*, pp. 74–81 (1993) (hereinafter E. van Donzel).
7 *Memoirs*, p. 87. As per Arab custom, her *surie* mother gained her freedom upon Sayyid Said's death, but did not inherit assets.
8 *Memoirs*, p. 202–3. The cargo was on the *Ilmedjidi*, also the subject of an endearing chapter in the *Letters*, pp. 66–70.

About the Addendum

The story of her first trip had made it into the *Memoirs*, when publication was delayed so that the travel account could be added as the last chapter. But her second trip came after publication, so an "addendum" (*Nachtrag*) for a reissued *Memoirs* made sense. What would have been contemporary history at the time is now almost a petty detail, but we can tell from her writing that the manner in which she was treated left her smarting for a good long while.[9] For all the official British and German accounts and opinions, I am glad we also have her side of the story.

———·•·———

Unlike other writings in this collection, I think we can safely call the *Addendum* a family project. We have not only Sayyida Salme's original draft, but also subsequent iterations. In fact, we have four versions, two from during her lifetime, both handwritten, and two from her children after she died, both typed, with photos of each on the next pages.[10]

In the original notebook, Sayyida Salme's bold, black strokes in the old German script course across the pages with an energy that matches the intensity of her memories and opinions. Added to her text is an overlay of edits, in pencil likely from her son Rudolph and in a fine pen from her daughter Rosa, as they honed their mother's writing. This harkens back to Rosa's earliest school days when she offered to draft a letter for her mother, whose German was still relatively new.[11] It is perhaps a familiar immigrant story, where the younger generation leapfrogs into the new language, while the older generation provides continuity with the old.

What we see next is a second notebook, this time in Rosa's even hand, with another overlay of edits, also presumed to be from her brother Rudolph. The young adults were still at it. This was an important piece of writing, the sequel to the saga, particularly regarding finances and inheritance. It was a chance to set the record straight, what with all the speculation, rumors, false reporting, and innuendo out there. Sensitive topics, lots of details—they clearly wanted to get it just right.

---

9 I cannot help but note that the German word "Nachtrag" has the same root as *nachtragen*, literally "to carry after." Among other definitions, the word is used to refer to someone who bears a grudge against someone else.
10 The handwritten notebooks are in the Leiden University Libraries at Or. 27.135 A1–2. The first typed version is in Alexander von Brand's private collection. See footnote 16 below for the second typed version.
11 "I told her what I was intending to write, and she, this eight-year-old, crafted the sentences better and more clearly than I could have done at the time." (*Letters*, p. 103)

The *Addendum* was, however, never published during Sayyida Salme's lifetime.[12] The family was unable to find anyone willing to reissue the *Memoirs*, to which the *Addendum* would have been appended. Interest in the Oriental princess had perhaps waned; times had moved on. In 1890, Germany had ceded its interest in Zanzibar and much of East Africa to the British in exchange for Heligoland (German *Helgoland*). Neither Sayyida Salme's marked edits in her copy of the 1886 *Memoirs*,[13] nor the complementary *Addendum* account with details from her 1888 trip, made it to the public.

Instead, after Sayyida Salme died in 1924, when more writings were found, her children first debated and then agreed to share the unpublished materials.[14] In addition to the *Addendum*, this consisted primarily of the surprise *Letters to the Homeland* manuscript, as well as a short piece on her time in Beirut.[15] The handwritten texts were all typed up, first in a version that is still well-preserved in the possession of my third cousin from Antonie's branch of the family, Alexander von Brand, and then in a somewhat cleaned-up version that the children used to solicit interest. Once again, however, no publisher was forthcoming. In the end, Rudolph sent the final package to numerous institutions, where it was left for later generations to discover.[16]

---

12 In fact, the *Addendum* was not published for another hundred years. The only publication before this one came as part of Professor van Donzel's English-language compilation under the translated title "Sequels to My Memoirs." E. van Donzel, pp. 511–22. The *Nachtrag* has never yet been published in German.
13 This copy resides in the Leiden University Libraries at NINO SR 613 a–b. These later edits are reflected in my translation of the *Memoirs*. See also "On Translating." (*Memoirs*, p. 254)
14 See *Letters*, page xxi.
15 See *Syrian Customs and Conventions* on pages 46–50 below.
16 This was the "Literary Estate" (see *Letters*, pp. 1 and 161–62), of which one set was presented to Christiaan Snouck Hurgronje, a family friend who founded the Oriental Institute in Leiden, now in the Leiden University Libraries at Or. 6281. Correspondence regarding distribution of the other sets to the Zanzibar and British Museums and the major Hamburg and Berlin public libraries, can be found at Or. 27.135 C8. Rudolph's large collection of books and other materials that he gave to the Oriental Institute in 1937 is now preserved as the Said-Ruete Archive at the Leiden University Libraries.

```
                                    Postmark 21 Mei '45
Rudolph S a i d - R u e t e    27, Kensington Court
                                WES 3664   LONDON  W.8

        I should be very much obliged  to hear
     if the LIBRARY has survived the war or what
     has become of same. I ask this as I intend to
     let you have a substantial amiunt of more books.
                    Anticipated thanks.
                                              RSR
   ontvangen 7 Juni '45
   en beantw.
```

An inquiry by Sayyida Salme's son about his collection a year before he died

Custom-made bookcase to house the Rudolph Said-Ruete collection

Pages from Sayyida Salme's original handwritten text, with edits by her children

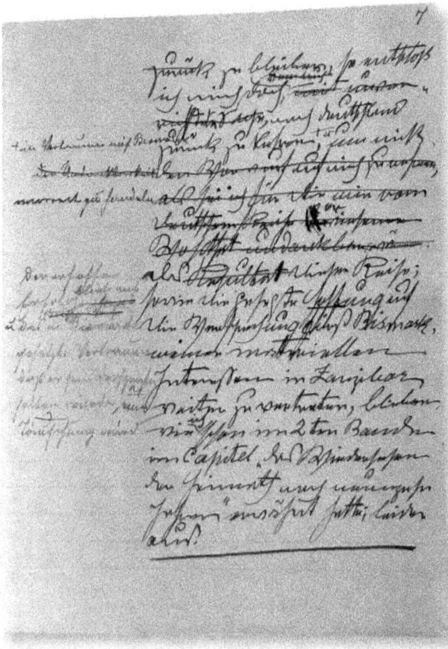

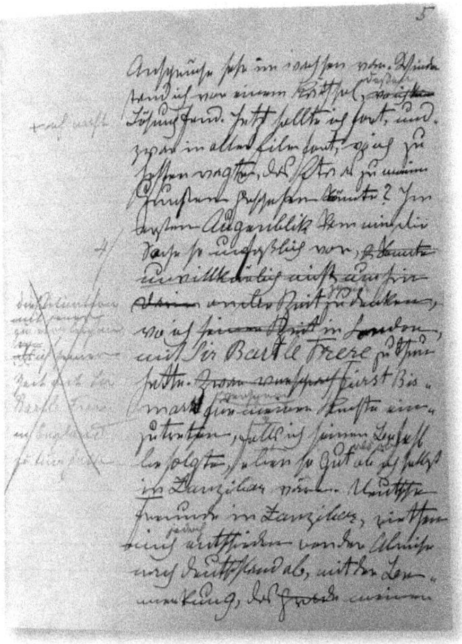

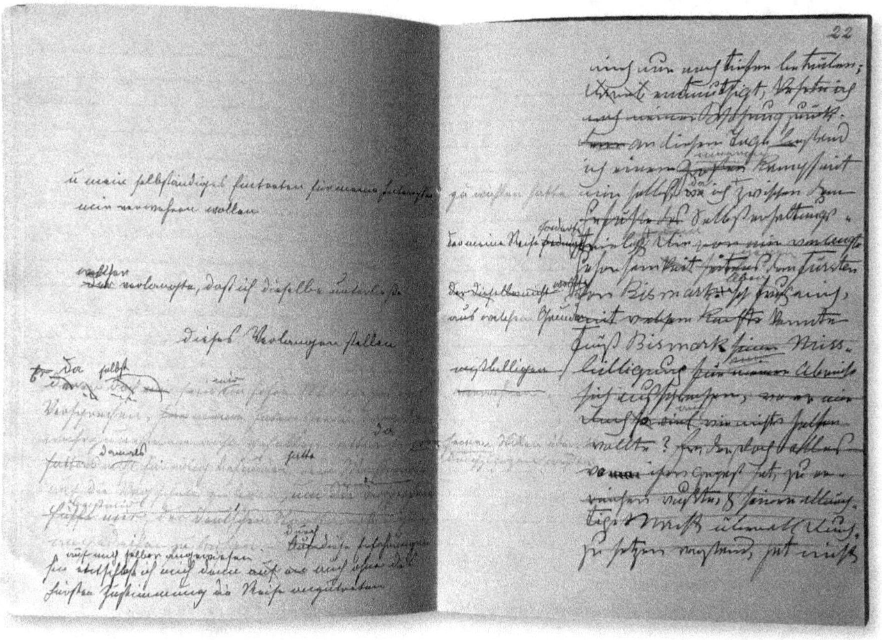

Pages from Sayyida Salme's text, after edits, as rewritten by her daughter Rosa

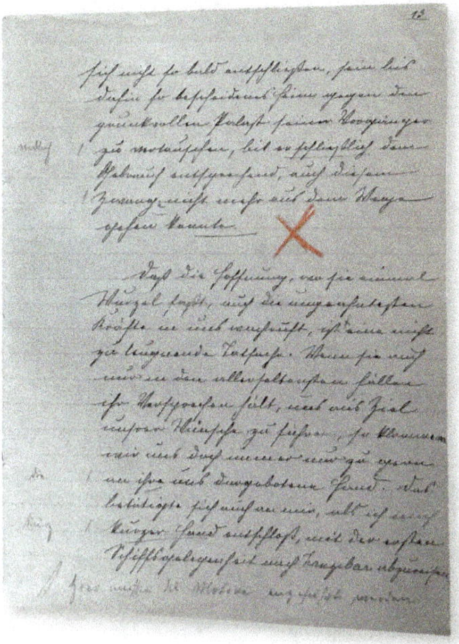

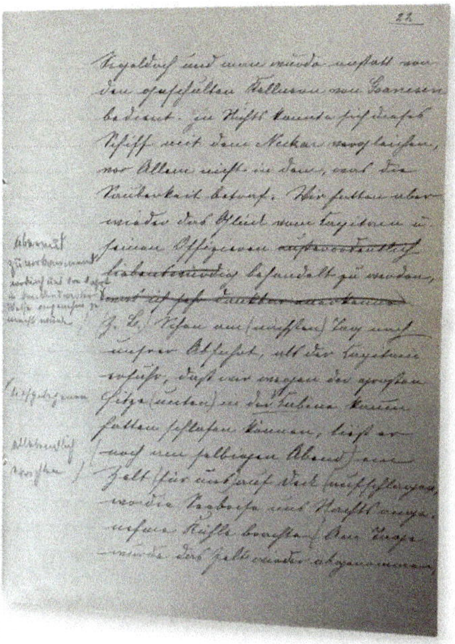

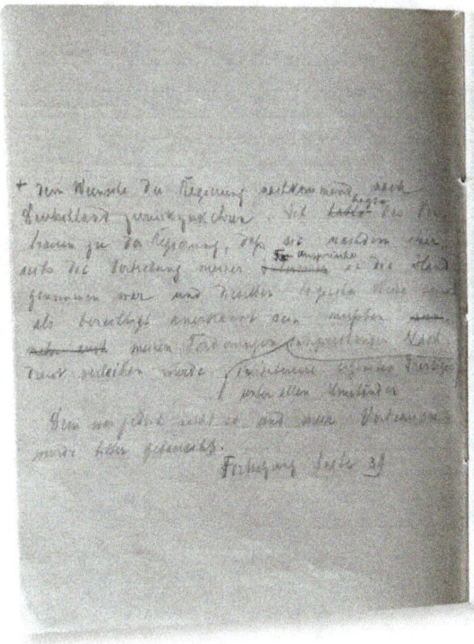

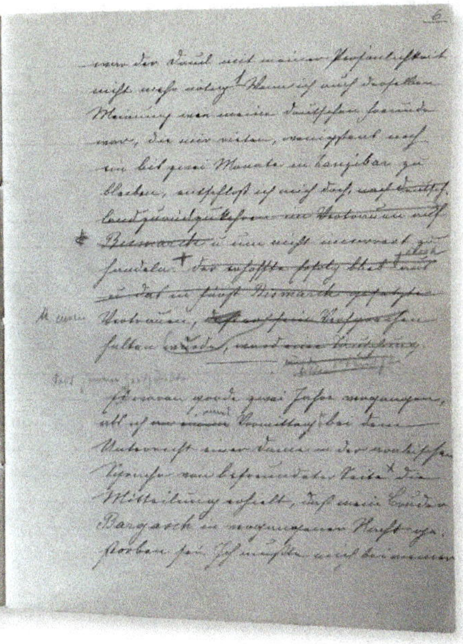

Nachtrag Zu Meinen Memoiren.

Mit einem Gedicht, das meine geliebte Schwester mir zugesandt hatte schlossich die Memoiren da sie, wie so viele bei uns, nur des Lesens aber nicht des Schreibens kundig war, liess sie mir dasselbe von einer gemeinsamen Freundin niederschreiben. Der klagende Ton in den einfachen Zeilen hatte seinen Zweck nicht verfehlt, denn er schlug auch bei mir tief empfundehe Saiten an. Betruebt wie sie selber bei meiner so ploetzlich beschlossenen Abreise war, ahnte sie nicht, wie viel mehr ich unter derselben litt. Auch konnte und durfte ich sie nicht mit den meiner Abreise bedingenden Umstaenden bekannt machen. Die Situation war so verwickelt,dass sie dieselbe kaum begriffen haben wuerde; auch waere ich Gefahr gelaufen mich in ihrer Auffasung herab zu setzen. Ich empfand eine Art Scham ueber meinen von Berlin aus befohlenen Rueckzug und vermied gern jegliche Mitteilung ueber denselben : denn sowohl die Meinen als auch die Bevoelkerung von Zansibar glaubten, dass die Ankunft des Geschwaders zu dem Zwecke erfolgt sei mich - die Deutsche Untertanin - bei der Geltendmachung ihrer Ansprueche zu unterstuetzen. Die Naturvoelker, denen es an Vestaendniss fuer die so meisterhaft geschulte Diplomatie des Abendlandes und ihrer Schachzuege mangelt, nahmen dies diese Erzaehlung fuer bare Muenze. Weshalb kam ich denn auch auf einen Regierungsdampfer in Begleitung des Geschwaders nach

First typewritten version of Sayyida Salme's manuscript

- 1 -

Nachtrag zu meinen Memoiren.
===

Mit einem Gedicht, das meine geliebte Schwester mir zugesandt hatte, schloss ich die Memoiren; da sie, wie so viele bei uns, nur des Lesens, aber nicht des Schreibens kundig war, liess sie mir dasselbe von einer gemeinsamen Freundin niederschreiben. Der klagende Ton in den einfachen Zeilen hatte seinen Zweck nicht verfehlt, denn er schlug auch bei mir tief empfundene Saiten an. Betrübt wie sie selber bei meiner so plötzlich beschlossenen Abreise war, ahnte sie nicht, wie viel mehr ich unter derselben litt. Auch konnte und durfte ich sie nicht mit den meine Abreise bedingenden Umständen bekannt machen. Die Situation war so verwickelt, dass sie dieselbe kaum begriffen haben würde, auch wäre ich Gefahr gelaufen, mich in ihrer Auffassung herabzusetzen. Ich empfand eine Art Scham über meinen von Berlin aus befohlenen Rückzug und vermied gern jegliche Mitteilung über denselben: denn sowohl die Meinen als auch die Bevölkerung von Zansibar glaubten, dass die Ankunft des Geschwaders zu dem Zwecke erfolgt sei, mich - die deutsche Untertanin - bei der Geltendmachung ihrer Ansprüche zu unterstützen. Die Naturvölker, denen es an Verständnis für die so meisterhaft geschulte Diplomatie des Abendlandes und ihrer Schachzüge mangelt, nahmen diese Erzählung für bare Münze. Weshalb kam ich denn auch auf einem Regierungsdampfer in Begleitung des Geschwaders nach Zansibar ? Man konnte nichts anderes glauben, als dass die Deutschen den Arabern zeigen wollten, dass sie gekommen waren, um ihrer Untertanin zu ihrem Rechte zu verhelfen. Diese Annahme fand seinerzeit nicht nur in meiner Heimat, sondern selbst in

Second typewritten version of Sayyida Salme's manuscript

Addendum to My Memoirs

I closed my memoirs with a poem that my beloved sister had sent me. Since she, like so many others back home, could only read and not write, she had had a common friend write it up for me. The plaintive tone in its simple lines did not miss their mark, for they struck deep chords in me as well. Distressed as she was by my abrupt decision to depart, she could not have divined how much more it made me suffer. Nor was I able or allowed to let her know the circumstances that compelled my exit. The situation was so convoluted that it would have been hard for her to comprehend, added to which I would have risked denigrating myself to her.

/[17] I felt a degree of shame about Berlin's command that I pull out and preferred to avoid any mention of it.[18] My loved ones, and all the Zanzibari population, believed that the arrival of the fleet of warships had been intended to support me—as a German subject—in asserting my claims. The indigenous people, who lack the capacity to understand the masterfully schooled diplomacy of the Occident and all its chess moves, accepted this tale at face value. Why else would I be traveling to Zanzibar on a government steamer under the escort of warships? There could be no reason other than the Germans wanting to show the Arabs that they were here to enforce the rights of their subject.

/This assumption prevailed not only in my homeland, but even in Germany, where many of my friends were filled with hope for my future. I will always gratefully recall their selfless love and concern for me. Because of this erroneous

---

17 The translator has inserted a number of paragraph breaks for greater readability, in each case denoted by "/."
18 Sayyida Salme is referring to the end of her first return trip to Zanzibar in 1885, when she visited the island under escort of a German naval fleet, as more fully described in the last chapter of her *Memoirs* (pp. 212–28).

Addendum to My Memoirs

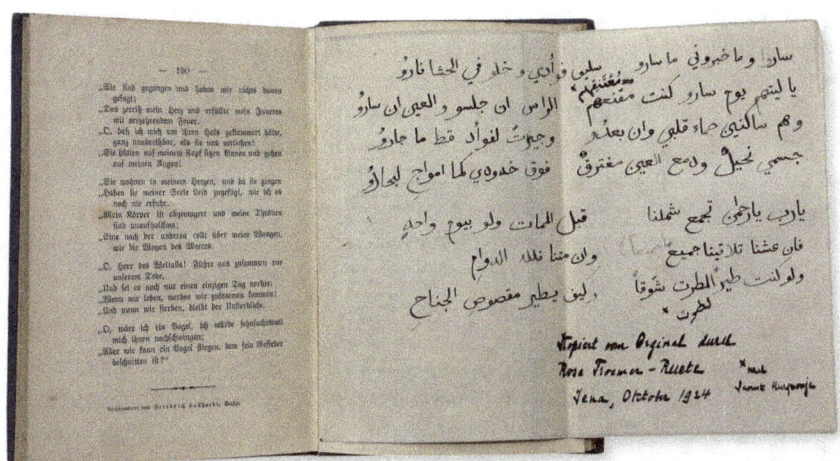

Arabic version of the poem at the end of the Memoirs, *handwritten by Rosa*

perception about the unfolding display of German power in the harbor of Zanzibar—presumed to represent my interests—I received numerous inquiries from my Arab acquaintances about applying to become part of the German Reich. It did not take long, however, for these gullible people to realize that their enthusiasm had been somewhat premature.

Prince Bismarck[19] had apparently deemed it prudent to call me back to Germany in view of the superior political maneuverings of the English toward Zanzibar. His instructions came completely out of the blue, just at a time when the prospects for realizing my material claims were very much on the upswing. I thus faced a conundrum I could not crack. I was to leave now, without delay, at the very moment that I finally dared hope things would shift in my favor. At first, I found the turn of events utterly incomprehensible, and I was sorely reminded of the disgraceful experiences I had been subjected to in England, courtesy of Sir Bartle Frere at the time.[20]

---

19 Otto Eduard Leopold von Bismarck (1815–98) was Chancellor of Germany at the time. He had received the title Prince in recognition of the victory over France in 1871 and then oversaw Germany's unification to become its first Chancellor, a position he held until 1890.

20 Sayyida Salme describes this English manipulation in her chapter "Sayyid Barghash in London" (*Memoirs*, pp. 205–10; and my commentary on p. 248). While seeking to exercise what she perceived as her rights, Sayyida Salme became a "pawn" in the colonial maneuverings of the time, both used and abused by the great powers. No country—neither Zanzibar, Germany, nor England—stepped in to treat her as a legitimate subject or showed her a worthy degree of responsibility. As she put it herself: "Every nation here is like a big institution, and its citizens are just the wards, naturally without them realizing it." (*Letters*, p. 116)

Prince Bismarck promised to pursue my rights, if I followed his instructions, as vigilantly as if I were in Zanzibar myself. Nevertheless, German friends in Zanzibar advised me emphatically against a return to Germany. They observed that my presence at exactly this moment portended success, in that the Sultan, as well as the English Consul General, had reached the conclusion that it would be preferable to placate me sooner than later. I had become uncomfortable for them through what appeared to be a validated interest on the part of my new homeland's government, which had even led to interpellations in the English parliament.

With my dismissal, it became clear to me that the German side had simply used me as a means to an end. Once the Sultan had met Germany's demands and seemed inclined to conclude a commercial treaty, the pressure of my presence was no longer needed. Although I shared the views of my German friends, who advised me to stay in Zanzibar at least another month or two, I ultimately decided to appease the government and return to Germany. I put my trust in the government, which, after having agreed to pursue my entitlements, must have logically considered them valid. I trusted that it would in any event give my claims due emphasis in the interest of its own prestige. And yet, this proved not the case, and my trust was bitterly betrayed.

/At the time, the newspapers spread the falsehood that I had returned to Germany in full possession of my inheritance, consisting of a bounty of no less than twenty-eight houses. That is completely false. Although five of my brothers, five sisters, my Aunt Aasche, three nieces, a nephew, and a very well-off stepmother have died in the time since Barghash became Sultan, and I am permitted to assert my claims to a portion of their estates, I have not received a penny. And my claims, which by now amount to several hundred thousand Marks, and which even the English Consul General declared legitimate—and that is certainly not insignificant—remain unanswered to this day.

/This fact remains the case, despite my brother's offer, as disclosed to me by the Foreign Ministry several months after my departure, to settle the aggregate of my claims with a one-time payment of 6,000 Rupees (approximately 9,800 Marks). Such a resolution of the efforts on my behalf has done nothing to demonstrate Germany's political strength at the start of its colonial endeavors. To the contrary: Today, after twenty years, even the insiders of the colonial movement have no doubt that our politics regarding Zanzibar, including the initial, deceitful saber rattling, reflect a record of exceptional ineptness. Prince Bismarck, after having already left the political stage a number of years earlier and reached the "dismal Treaty of Helgoland"—as he himself described it to my son during a visit to Friedrichsruh[21]—was apparently also convinced that our engagement in East Africa was severely lacking in purposeful energy and vision.

/I immediately declined the amount offered to me by my rich brother, which represented but a small fraction of the lavish gifts with which he sent the representatives entrusted with German interests on their way. As such, I believed to have made my brother aware that, despite all the vagaries of life, my pride was still intact. And yet, sometime later, I coincidentally discovered that my intention had rested on a false assumption, for the sum in question had been inexplicably deposited in the Foreign Ministry's general account. By this time, my brother had died. Rather humiliating for me, he will have departed from this life with the impression that my claims had been satisfied with this scant sum. There was no way to rectify this misimpression, and since I had no reason after all these experiences to allow the slush fund of Germany's foreign affairs to accrue new amounts in such an odd and uncontested manner, I reclaimed the amount on behalf of my children, which was then promptly put at my disposal, together with interest on the interest.

Two years had just passed after my return to Berlin when I was giving Arabic lessons to a lady and received word from a friend that my brother Barghash had passed away in the night. I had to excuse myself to my student and cut the lesson short. How could I have continued teaching under those circumstances! That was completely out of the question, heavily affected as I was by the news that had reached me. In this moment, any bitterness toward the deceased disappeared. Before my soul stood only the picture of the merry companion of my youth, this hot-blooded youngster, and next to him, the picture of my unforgettable sister Chole, as she pleaded with me at the time, with her tearful, soulful eyes, that I not desert her so very beloved brother in his distress, but rather stand by him in his difficult position. These and similar thoughts of my youth overtook me completely, and even though it was impossible for me to suddenly forget all that I had had to endure in the past eighteen years, the harshest of all from Barghash, I nonetheless forgave my dead brother everything in that moment.

/I gave my spirit wings that day and hurried far over the seas to the beloved shores of the homeland, where today the earthly shell of the ruler of Zanzibar was being laid to rest, among the very mixed feelings of the relatives and

---

21 Friedrichsruh became Chancellor Bismarck's residence as a gift from Emperor William I following Germany's victory over France and unification in 1871.

population. Even there it will be said: Le Roi est mort, vive le Roi!²²

/How many people will have seen their secret hopes irrevocably dashed, and yet, how many others will have seen their quietly harbored desires suddenly sprout? Such is the way of the world. The camarilla that Barghash had so favored—and are they not everywhere?—will naturally complain, while the poor downtrodden in their unseen quarters will sing songs of praise in their souls. Who could blame them? It is, of course, human! Even the otherwise humane and very beloved ex-Minister Abdalla il Shachsi, for example, had felt himself compelled on this day, against all customs and conventions, to hoist a flag at his home, as a sign of—his joy.

/Our house rules always call for the oldest male member of the family to be the successor to the deceased Sultan. As such, a son may rise to the throne only if no older brothers or nephews of the Sultan are still alive. In this case, Chalife was the legally determined successor to Barghash as his oldest brother, and not Barghash's son Chalid.²³ Nothing in this whole wide world could have been more undesirable to Chalife, this poor, much plagued and much pursued, man, than to have to step up to this legacy. Worn out in body and soul, nothing lay further from his mind than to covet this honor (compare Volume 2, page 179).²⁴

I learned later that my brother Barghash had returned deathly ill on a trip from Oman to Zanzibar at six o'clock in the evening and had then died the very same night at one o'clock in the morning. He had had high hopes of improving his health on this trip, but must nonetheless have felt the end nearing, as he bade the captain to push full speed ahead back to Zanzibar, so that he could die amidst his family. And so he did arrive in Zanzibar just hours before his death. Immediately after he died, the news was rushed to Chalife to inform him of the event.

/Chalife was on one of his plantations at the time and unaware that Barghash had returned at sunset, much less was no longer among the living. When the messenger reached him toward morning—it was still very dark—and had him

---

22 Written in French in the original, this means "The king is dead; [long] live the king!"
23 Chalid later attempted to take his turn at being Sultan, but, courtesy of the British, it did not go well. See, e.g., "Sayyida Khalid Bin Barghash, Britain and the Throne of Zanzibar" by B. Saud Turki, in *Anaquel de Estudios Árabes*, Vol. 21, pp. 35-53 (2021).
24 This page reference is to the second volume of the original *Memoiren*, at the end of the book, where Sayyida Salme describes how the newly ascended Sultan Barghash threw his next-in-line Chalife into the dungeon—for no known reason—where he lay in chains for three years. (*Memoirs*, p. 224)

woken to present the news, Chalife refused to believe the message, thinking this was instead some underhanded trick. Abused by much unfair treatment in the past, the poor, skittish man did not trust this nighttime visit and at first kept the messenger from coming forward. Once, however, he was finally convinced of the verity of the matter, he is said to have called out that he had no wish to become Sultan, that this honor should go to his younger brother. When in the end he had no choice but to take on this designated role, which he also later always considered a burden, he had a hard time making the switch to the pompous palace of his predecessors in lieu of his until-then so humble home. But ultimately, he conformed to custom when he could no longer avoid the obligation.

———•·———

It is an undeniable fact that hope, once it takes root, also awakens in us the most unexpected strength. Even if it keeps its promise only in the rarest cases to lead us to our desired goal, we still love to cling to its outstretched hand. That was confirmed in my case as well, when I decided on the spot to leave for Zanzibar on the first ship to sail. I firmly believed that, with the death of my hostile brother, I would encounter no difficulties reconnecting with my relatives and receiving my inheritance for the benefit of my children. I had no time to spare if I wanted to catch the next ship due into Aden, which, coming from Bombay, headed to Zanzibar every four weeks. And so, the next days were filled with very much to do, very much to consider. Above all, we had to sell some stocks to free up the travel cash.—

/I felt I should inform the Foreign Ministry of my travel plans to avoid later misinterpretations, thus also using the opportunity to request the good will of the German government. I believed Germany would now have an easier time supporting my pecuniary claims than was the case three years earlier during the naval display towards Zanzibar. Back then, it was Barghash who, in his diplomatic calculations, had put obstacles in the way. Now that he was no longer living, there should be little impediment to recognizing my modest inheritance claims. Added to that, here I was, the widow of a German, who, in the eighteen years since the death of my husband, had fought my way through all the heartaches and hardship of life with my three children. I considered this request to be self-evident and justified.

/My interest in speaking with the Foreign Secretary at the time, Count Herbert Bismarck, was not granted. To the contrary, I received notice that Prince Bismarck did not condone my trip to Zanzibar, naturally without giving any rhyme or reason why. This rejection, so categorical and without any clarification, only served to heighten my grief. Deeply disheartened, I fought a great fight within myself during these days, with the choice between my own survival instinct that called for travel and my obedience to Prince Bismarck that commanded me to let it go. But, I now asked myself, on what basis could he make this demand and deny me the ability to independently stand up for my own interests? It had been him, who knew only too well how to exert his power, that had considered it unnecessary in 1885 to tip the balance and assert his will in order to give me, a German citizen, the support that had been firmly pledged.

/Recalling that experience, and left to rely only on myself, I opted to move ahead with the trip without the Prince's endorsement. I would have liked my son to come along, so he could support and help me on the long trip. As a cadet who was just about to enter the army, my son was back then already at an age when he could not leave his fatherland without permission of the authorities. I therefore returned to the Foreign Ministry and requested that he be given some leave, with the commitment that he would return to Germany within six months. But this request, too, was categorically denied. Rather than assistance, I once again encountered only repudiation and hard-heartedness. And so, it was clear to me that Germany, in which I had previously placed my trust, was leaving me helplessly to my fate.

/With all this, I could not help but feel skeptical about the word "humanity," a word so widely used in Germany. I told myself that, although the theory was mostly admirable, the practice was anything but. The same applies to much-lauded freedom. In my case, too, it was just "yes, commoner, that is something completely different!" The broad stroke that was hitting me at that moment looked rather much like an act of despotism. Three years ago, when Prince Bismarck considered it useful to have my person present in Zanzibar, he had allowed my son to come along. But why not now? Did they perhaps fear my relatives were so simple-minded that they would attribute political motives to me about my son? There could be no greater error, since my relatives are nowhere near so dumb as to have a completely unauthorized ruler forced upon them, especially considering they have so many of their own pretenders in their midst.

/During my stay in London in 1875, when I sought support from the English government vis-à-vis the Sultan, they referred me to Germany as my second homeland, and not without justification. We can see, however, how far that got me. Germany left me on my own, as did England at the time.

Addendum to My Memoirs

It was the spring of 1888 when I left Berlin for Genoa, with my youngest daughter[25] instead of my son, to meet up with a ship of the Norddeutscher Lloyd[26] that would take us to Aden. Once on board, we ran into German acquaintances who were also headed for Zanzibar and proved most engaging and agreeable. The captain and his officers were also exceptionally kind to us, so that we were very well cared for. The trip progressed splendidly. We reached Aden in the late evening and then had to be shipped out to continue our travels on the steamer due in from Bombay. The captain had the ship's band perform a farewell tune for us. Even after we had gone a long distance, a very long distance towards shore, we could still see the white handkerchiefs waving us on our way. We were really very sad to leave the hospitable *Neckar*.

/We spent several days in Aden before the steamer from the British-India Company finally appeared, and we immediately made our way to the ship. What we found was completely different from the *Neckar*. Meals were eaten on deck under a tarp because of the heat and were served by Goans, instead of polished waiters. Nothing on this ship could live up to the *Neckar*, least of all its cleanliness. Then again, we were fortunate that the captain and his officers completely catered to our needs, which thankfully made the trip quite comfortable. Already the day after we took off, when the captain heard that we had hardly slept because of the great heat in our low-lying cabins, he had a tent pitched on the deck every evening, where we enjoyed the cooling sea breeze.

/Upon arriving in Mombasa, the friendly captain brought us to shore in his boat. As it happened to be Sunday, we went to church. I was surprised to hear a local African pastor give such an impressive sermon in Swahili. Everything here looked neat and clean under the caring administration of the English. There is absolutely no denying that wherever the English get a foothold, they spare neither effort nor cost to lift up the country in every respect. One need not look far for proof; just consider Egypt. In colonial matters, the English are a nation that—in contrast to its many rivals and thus accounting for its dominant position—engages in healthy, purposeful politics.

---

25 This was Rosalie, also known as Rosa, the translator's great-grandmother.
26 The Norddeutscher Lloyd, known as the Bremen Line, was founded in 1857 and grew rapidly with the increase of transatlantic trade and migrant flows after the U.S. Civil War. The carrier began traveling east in mid-1886 under a contract with the German government to serve as a mail line to China and Australia. According to records posted by Norway-Heritage Hands Across the Sea, the *Neckar* traveled from Bremen to Hong Kong, where it arrived on May 18, 1888. In subsequent years, the company lost its entire seafaring fleet at the end of World War I, and again during World War II, before merging with the Hamburg-America Line in 1970 to become HAPAG-Lloyd, currently the fourth biggest shipping line in the world—which Norddeutscher Lloyd had also become by its 25th anniversary in 1882.

The ship that took Sayyida Salme and her daughter Rosa to Aden in 1888

We also put in a call at Lamu[27] and took a short excursion onto the island. When we wanted to return to deck, we found the ocean completely changed. The tide had set in with such force that massive waves were pounding the shore. With utmost effort and delay, we finally reached the ship as the last to arrive, and it immediately powered up to head out. Since it is not customary to wait for tardy passengers, and ships are meticulous in maintaining their departure times, I apologized to the captain for our involuntary lateness. And yet, he was kind enough to respond in his simple manner that he would have waited for us in any case.

From Lamu, we continued directly to Zanzibar. The joy of seeing my beloved homeland again was not as straightforward this time. I was aware that, in pursuing my goal, some hurdles would lie in my way. I nonetheless considered it my duty to spare no effort in championing my rightful portion of the inheritance from the estates of my deceased relatives. Not that I even remotely indulged any sanguine hopes; that was dispelled by all my many dismal experiences of the past. There is no contesting the fact that in the

---

27 Lamu became a UNESCO World Heritage Site in 2001 as "the oldest and best-preserved Swahili settlement in East Africa," which also features much Arab, Persian, Indian, and European influence. The period under Omani protection, when Sayyid Said bin Sultan, Sayyida Salme's father, answered Lamu's appeal to fend off the Mazrui rebels from the Kenyan coast, is considered Lamu's golden age. Meanwhile, a report from 2010 found that Lamu was one of a dozen worldwide sites most "on the verge . . . [of] irreparable loss and damage" (out of 500 surveyed). "Saving Our Vanishing Heritage: Safeguarding Endangered Cultural Heritage Sites in the Developing World," Global Heritage Foundation (2010).

Addendum to My Memoirs

Orient, and even more so in the Occident, questions of money are among the most uncomfortable topics that one could even contemplate. This fact may not, however, mislead those who have been harmed to remain passive in the pursuit of their legal claims. Only after the battle has been lost may one lay down arms, not before.

We had only just arrived in Zanzibar when I had to take note that the local German Consul displayed a less than obliging attitude towards me. The gentleman in question was a complete stranger to me, such that his animosity could not have been personal, but had to be of a much more political nature. I mention this explicitly to indicate the state of relations. I had traveled to my homeland fully cognizant of my status as a German subject, and I presented myself as such.

/From my inner circle, I learned that my brother, Sultan Chalife, who spent most of his time outside of the city, was very favorably disposed towards me and also often took my side among his other relatives. This news emboldened me to try to reach a reconciliation with my loved ones. Meanwhile, it must have become very obvious to everyone the degree to which the German Consul, upon whose goodwill I depended for reaching my objective, not only avoided us on every occasion, but apparently even slighted us relative to all other Germans.

/This behavior left my relatives completely baffled. They believed the German Consul must have his reasons for being so dismissive of me. To my mind, however, the matter was clear. I knew to a certainty that I had become subject to Bismarck's caprice. Having embarked on my travels without his consent, I was to be ignored by the representative of the German Reich. What that meant for me, he surely would have known. All my relatives concurred: Let the German Consul step in for you and take up your cause, for only then can something be undertaken for a German subject. They were right, and my desolation became doubly palpable.

/Ashamed on the outside and deeply wounded on the inside, I believed I had one last step to take before giving up hope forever. I decided to write to the German Emperor[28] and bid him to relieve the cause of my distress with a

---

28 By then, it was Kaiser Wilhelm II (1859–1941), the last German Emperor and King of Prussia. He had only recently stepped up to this role in June 1888 at the age of 29, after succeeding his father's 99-day reign. In March 1890, he effectively dismissed the much older Chancellor Bismarck and then ruled directly until abdicating with the loss of World War I in 1918.

merciful word. I also wrote Prince Bismarck at the same time, in which I implored him yet again not to withhold his benevolence, if only to preserve Germany's reputation among my fellow countrymen. I found myself in a situation that truly was not to be envied. As I extended this request to the Prince, I convinced myself that it would be all but impossible for such a great man as Bismarck to avenge himself in such a petty manner by continuing to deny a helpless lady her rightful protection.

/In the meantime, there was no end to the questions from my friends about why the German government was so clearly deserting me. Yes, why?! As the weeks and months passed with no response to my letters, my hopes of achieving anything through Germany died off forever. Denied any closure, I had no choice but to leave.

———•———

Whether this undeserved treatment that was bestowed on me was well-suited to elevating Germany's prestige in Zanzibar is something I cannot judge. It occurred at a time, while I was there, when Germany began to introduce various reforms in East Africa and expanded the tax system. Every coconut palm was to be taxed one Mark per year, which led to loud grumbling on the part of local Arabs. Many came to seek my advice. When I explained that I had nothing to do with these things, and they would better seek out the German Consul, they responded: Who can help and understand us better than you, who knows our customs and conventions better than all the Germans in East Africa put together, since you also speak their language and are well-versed in their affairs unlike any of us.—The following years have, of course, shown how little the people in German East Africa were able to befriend the one-sided military regiment.

Before now leaving my homeland forever, I entered once more into a period that was very amply filled with inner conflict. My siblings and relatives felt great compassion for me, and they beseeched me to become theirs again, to return to the old faith of my fathers and turn my back on the Germans. "Come, be ours again, for you belong to us! Do not go back to those strangers, but stay here with your family. You have our sacred promise that you will have a good life with us. But as long as you turn away from us and attach yourself to other people and their faith, we will never be in a position to freely support you."

/For weeks, yes months, I was forced to listen to these and similar words with a torn heart. Most gripping of all was when my sister Z.,[29] since passed away, begged me to give in and stay with them. How I fought within myself to hear her words, only my God knows. I openly admit that I was often at the edge of my resolve, and naught but the thought of my children, who had been born and raised in the European way, kept me from succumbing to their pleas and staying with them in the beloved homeland. I valued the wellbeing of my children above my own happiness. Under no circumstances, not even for the most shining prospects, was I willing to sacrifice the emotional equilibrium of my children.

In the fall, we set off to depart, but there was no way for me to return to Germany after having been so aggrieved. We chose Palestine as our next destination. For proper appearances, we traveled from Zanzibar to Port Said in first class, but since low tide had set into my cashbox with a vengeance, I considered it necessary to travel second class with my daughter along the Syrian coast, where no one would know me. In Port Said, we embarked on a ship of the Messageries Maritime[30] headed for Jaffa. The next morning, as we were strolling back and forth on deck, the captain came to us and began to converse. It did not take long for him to pose the less than delicate question of why we were not traveling first class. I looked with surprise at this good man, whom I had until now never before seen. He took note of my astonishment and hurried to explain that he had learned of my identity, probably from the ship agent in Port Said. He was a former officer of the French Marine and had thus gotten to know Oman and Zanzibar, also knew my nephew, the Sultan of Oman, and my brother, the Sultan of Zanzibar, from whom he had received various tokens.—Such encounters were least desirable at this time, but fate unfortunately does not care much about our feelings. The captain was kind enough to invite us to tea with him in the first class, but I thanked him and declined.

About a year later, I received a visit in Jaffa from the former physician of my brother Barghash, a highly educated, amiable gentleman, who spoke

---

29 We have no record of which sister this was, but it may have been Zemzem, who had grown close to Sayyida Salme when they both lived on their plantations in the countryside. (*Memoirs*, p. 98)

30 This French shipping company, also known as MesMar, thrived on the Mediterranean Sea during this time, with ports of call from Marseille to Malta, across to Alexandria, and up to Constantinople.

practically all the cultured languages perfectly. He told me that when my *Memoirs* appeared in 1886, and my brother learned about the book, Barghash had ordered him to translate it word for word. When I asked if he had also dared to translate the chapter "Said [sic][31] Barghash in London" (Volume II, page 146), he confirmed that he had had to do this as well, and indeed, this chapter had interested Barghash the most. This gentleman also assured me that my brother had even voiced a good bit of praise about the *Memoirs*. That took me very much by surprise, for I must admit, I had rather expected the opposite.

/What must Barghash have felt when taking up my *Memoirs*, to see such a book written by his sister, of which he was unable to decipher a single word beyond my Arabic signature. Did he think back to the time when I, in my youth, took up my Arabic pen in his service?[32] Very possibly! And since then? What all has happened between then and now! For me, beyond measure!

---

31 This is an error in the typed manuscript. The chapter title in the original German is "Sejjd Bargasch in London," referring to his appellation "Sayyid" as Sultan. Sayyida Salme used the same title for the father as "Sejjid Saîd" in the first chapter of her *Memoiren*. The "Said" error noted here confuses the proper name with the title, probably because they sound the same. "Sejjid" means Sultan and "Saîd" is the first name of the father, not of Barghash. To add to the confusion, Barghash's father's full name was Sayyid Said bin Sultan, where Sultan was, in fact, the first name of his father, Sayyid Sultan bin Ahmed. "Bin" means "son of." In sum, Barghash was a Sayyid, but was not named Said, even though his father was both. Barghash's full name was Sayyid Barghash bin Said. Got it?

32 Acting in support of Barghash's attempted coup, "I, the youngest female member of the conspiracy, became what was effectively the general secretary of the alliance because I was able to write and thus expected to handle all correspondence with the chieftains." *Memoirs*, p. 178.

Shoreline view of Stonetown in 1847, with the Zanzibari red flag waving

Beach view of the Adler, *the German ship that took Sayyida Salme to Zanzibar*

ABOUT SYRIAN CUSTOMS AND CONVENTIONS

Sayyida Salme left only a few tantalizing pages about a place where she lived much of her life, and we could wish for more. We do not know exactly when she wrote these pages, except that it must have been after 1892,[33] when she took up residence in Beirut. It is also not clear whether the children knew about this handwritten text before she died, but likely not, since the wide left margin, ready for edits, is blank.[34] Fortunately, however, the contents of this black notebook made their way into the collected writings that the children had typed up after her death, as part of her "literary estate."[35] It gives me an excuse to say a few things about this third chapter of her life.

From 1889 to 1914, the eastern shore of the Mediterranean Sea, first Jaffa, then Beirut, was her home.[36] That was a quarter century, close to a third of her life, even though Sayyida Salme is almost always associated with Zanzibar and Germany. Of course, we mostly know her through her own writings, the *Memoirs* that describe her young life in Zanzibar, and the *Letters* that describe her early days in Germany. There is no equivalent third book to publish about her older, wiser years, the denouement after the plot twists.

As she had done with Zanzibar and Germany in two prior manuscripts, it appears that Sayyida Salme still had the same instinct to describe the time, place, and people in her new location. With her customary bold strokes, she started to lend her ethnographic lens to Syrian society, but then got no further. It is a pity for us that she did not keep going, but I would like to think that it was good for her. To me, it means she had a busy and fulfilled life in Beirut, without the need to dig around in her experiences. It may signal that she was more content in her new setting, no longer feeling the need to dispel misconceptions or rectify the record. It may be that the fervor to recount had receded. For the first time, she was no longer the outsider looking in, but comfortably becoming an insider. With respect to Beirut, it may have made that distancing, scrutinizing lens harder to position.

---

33 The Leiden University Libraries guide for the Said-Ruete collection (ubl649) suggests circa 1895.
34 Compare this to the intensive editing by Rosa and Rudolph of the *Addendum* (pages 16–19 above).
35 Now located at the Leiden University Libraries Or. 27.135 A6.
36 Sayyida Salme left Zanzibar in November 1888 and was so done with both Zanzibar and Germany that she headed straight to Jaffa, where there was a strong German presence. In 1892, she made the move to Beirut, both of her daughters still with her. E. van Donzel, pp. 95–97. Beirut was the capital of a Syrian province (*vilayet*) at the time and did not become part of Lebanon until after World War I.

Her second trip to Zanzibar in 1888 had also left her spent.[37] She may have needed the years that followed to regroup and re-energize. In the relative comfort of her new life, she now also had time and space to delve into her past. These were presumably the years when she filled the three notebooks, more than 600 pages, that she called *Briefe nach der Heimat*—the *Letters* I mention above. Harkening back to such a hard time was no doubt also hard to do. Even if it was cathartic, it surely also took an emotional toll. Her third *Briefe* notebook ends rather abruptly, like running out of steam after all those pages.[38] Her Syrian reflections appear to have had a similar fate after only a few pages.

As far as my own translations of her work, it would have been easy enough to leave out this fragment of an essay. Like a sketch on a napkin, it does not seem to be a serious piece of anything. She might have edited one or the other passage if she had gone back to hone her thinking or sought to create a more coherent narrative. So why include it here?

I think of these pages as a placeholder, a proxy for all that she did not write. In pointing to a portion of her life that was not captured by her pen, the message is in the silence. On the one hand, we can appreciate what she did write all the more. It is simply not normal for someone in her place to have written hundreds and hundreds of pages. On the other hand, the fact that she stayed in Beirut as long as she did, leaving only when age and circumstances meant it was time, speaks for itself.

So what might she be saying with the blank rest of the notebook that never got written? What made Beirut such a comfortable place? I can just feel the relief in her silence. She had found a liminal space, finally a place where she was not forced to be "either/or," but could be "and."[39] Oriental in heart, Occidental in mind; Muslim in sensibility, Christian in belief; not a Zanzibari, Omani, or German as much as an amalgamation—a cosmopolitan citizen of the world. When she found Beirut, the city was becoming the new Constantinople.[40]

---

37 This seems evident in what Rosa wrote her brother Rudolph after the trip: "Mama is no longer the person she was when she left Berlin last April, the robust nature that could until then defy all storms. Our dear mother has suffered severely from the latest events, and her health has become more delicate." Ibid., p. 95.
38 See the essay "On Fear." (*Letters*, pp. 135–39)
39 See more in my very first blog post, "The Liminal In-Between," at www.sayyidasalme.com/blog.
40 As she says: "Had I, for example, been born and raised in Constantinople or Cairo, where European culture made inroads long ago, I may not have found such a stark contrast between Occident and Orient.... Should fate ever destine another Mohammedan from Constantinople or Cairo to be transplanted to Europe under the same circumstances as me, she would not even remotely be subjected to the same upheaval I have had to undergo. Had I not, until then, still been wearing the clothes of my great-ancestors from a thousand years ago and used my five fingers as natural knives and forks." (*Letters*, pp. 31–32)

And perhaps best of all, here she could live a rather normal life, without the extremes, neither in royalty, nor poverty.

Sayyida Salme spent her time in Beirut during a pocket of prosperity—a sweet spot when Beirut was thriving as a vibrant port city, a nexus between Europe and Arabia. Its bustling trade and mix of commerce, culture, and complexions must have felt very familiar to her, reminiscent of Zanzibar's heyday in her youth. Under the stable and savvy reign of her father, the great Sayyid Said bin Sultan, from 1806 to 1856, Zanzibar had become everyone's portal to and from East Africa. No one, it was said, went to the interior without passing through Stone Town—for money, supplies, the latest news, and whatever else. As much as we rightly recognize and criticize that this boom was built on the backs and lives of slaves, the rest of the world was in on it, seeking the spoils and making out hand over fist. As with Zanzibar, though, in Beirut the prosperity also ate itself and did not last.

Before jumping to her departure, we can hold onto what made a place like Beirut at the turn of the century so special, especially for someone like Sayyida Salme. Living as a single woman was still unconventional, but Beirut flourished as an intellectual hub that began to see the promotion of basic women's rights, like respect and autonomy, that was also trending in the West and other cosmopolitan centers.[41] She would have had one foot firmly in the traditional Arab culture, especially with her native Arabic as the dominant local language, and another foot among the Western-influenced, educated elite. And she was even well-practiced in straddling the two.

Beirut offered a dynamic cultural scene that surely appealed to someone like her, who had been so interested in science[42] and was, by then, an acclaimed author. As her daughter Rosa wrote, she was appreciated for her beautiful Arabic script.[43] She likely participated in educational offerings. We can even imagine that she was an excellent role model for others trying to meld Eastern

---

41 An apropos example is the literary magazine *The Woman's World*, begun in 1886 and edited by Oscar Wilde part-time from 1887–1889 (after he had the name changed from *The Lady's World*). It included Wilde's review of the 1888 Ward & Downey translation of the *Memoirs*, in which he noted: "No one who is interested in the social position of women in the East should fail to read these pleasantly-written memoirs. The Princess is herself a woman of high culture, and the story of her life is as instructive as history, and as fascinating as fiction" (pp. 229–31, 1888). Available online from the University of Minnesota.
42 *Letters*, pp. 87–88.
43 E. van Donzel, p. 97.

and Western influences. And yet, she probably did not stick out like a sore thumb. Unlike Rudolstadt, where the gossip had reveled in her every detail, or Stone Town, where she had become a larger-than-life personality, Beirut was both too large to care and small enough to give her a community that did.[44]

This carried over into Beirut's religious mix as well, where Muslims, Christians, Druze, and Jews all had their place. For someone whose faith remained essential to her being,[45] Sayyida Salme found access to a ready-made religious community. As she settled into Jaffa and Beirut, two and three decades after first setting foot in the West, it seems Christianity had matured to become a part of her. She was no longer a "poor Christian,"[46] but had evolved in her relationship to God and the church. The road had not been easy, and it corresponded to an evolution on many fronts. Already when she was writing her *Memoirs*, a decade or so after her arrival in Hamburg, we sense some distancing from her cultural groundings; she is seeing the sacrificial rituals and soothsaying spectacles in a different way.

With the tide lifting all boats, Christians in Beirut did well back then, increasing both their wealth and social standing. Protestants were in the minority compared to Catholics, but had a prominent presence in intellectual, educational, and social circles. Sayyida Salme found her community in the *Evangelische Kirche* (the German Protestant church) that was started in 1856. She also found two very close Christian friends in Paul Schröder, who was the German Consul in Beirut from 1896 to 1909, and his wife. The two families continued to be close friends into the next generation, when they all ended up back in Germany.[47] That Sayyida Salme was an integral part of the church community is also reflected in Rudolph's sponsorship of an altar at the *Evangelische Kirche* in his mother's memory.[48]

Not until 1914 did Sayyida Salme return to Germany, when she moved in with her youngest daughter Rosa, my great-grandmother. Many others were leaving Beirut at the time. Although we know few specifics about Sayyida Salme's life

---

44 Citizenship was also no issue, as the Ottoman Empire gave special privileges to many Europeans, including Germans, in negotiated "capitulations" that put them under consular jurisdiction. Her son Rudolph was even posted to the German consulate in Syria for a year in 1894. Because Germany had good relations with the Ottoman Empire, German nationals also faced less scrutiny than other nationals, especially as World War I neared.
45 See the translator's essay "On Faith" at pages 54–75 below.
46 This description of herself was later crossed out in her marked copy of the *Memoirs*. See pages 58–59 below.
47 See the photo on page 92 below. One of the Schröder daughters, Hedi, became the godmother of one of my aunts, and a Schröder granddaughter got to know my parents around 2000 when they lived for a time in Brazil.
48 See footnote 85 below.

in the Levant, nor what specifically motivated her to leave, history records what was going on around her. The end of the nineteenth century was a time of both ferment and volatility. The prosperity that brought in Western influence, that let Beirut blossom into a worldly city, also became a source of agitation. As businesses grew their heft and countries jockeyed for influence, the power balance started shifting. With the Young Turk revolution in 1908, Turkification increasingly clashed with Arab nationalism, and the Empire clamped down with martial law, arrests, executions, and other militarization. By now, the power balance was destabilizing. Local Christians made common cause with Muslim activists in a shared quest for autonomy, as Western influence continued to shape ideas of national identity and reform. The discontent with outside Ottoman rule turned even more toxic after the Empire aligned with Germany and Austria at the start of World War I. And politics were only part of it. The spring of 1915 brought an onslaught of locusts. Coming at the same time as the Allied maritime blockade at the start of World War I, the result was an absolutely debilitating famine.[49]

Whatever prompted Sayyida Salme to leave Beirut in 1914, it was a good time to be gone. By then, she was seventy years old, having lived a longer life than most of her half-siblings who had been born into the Sultan's harem, a time and place that must have seemed worlds away and an eternity ago. Times had greatly changed in those seventy years. As her end drew nearer, and the world grew madder, Sayyida Salme no doubt saw the benefits of having family around. No matter where in the world, the next years promised to be dark and difficult.

———•———

So now I have written even more than the Syrian text that she wrote. I hope only to amplify her words.

---

[49] The tragedy of these and other conflating factors is exhumed in detail in M. Tanielian's 2012 dissertation, "The War of Famine: Everyday Life in Wartime Beirut and Mount Lebanon (1914–1918)."

Rosa (Ghuza), Sayyida Salme's youngest daughter, in traditional attire

Notebook containing Sayyida Salme's handwritten essay on her time in Syria

-1-

<u>Syrische Sitten und Gebraeuche.</u>

Die Stadt Beyrut liegt sehr mahlerisch hingestreckt; umgeben von dem hohen Libanon und bespuelt vom Mittel-Laendischen Meer macht sie auf den Ankoemmling einen hoechst angenehmen Eindruck. Die vom Norden oder Sueden kommenden Schiffe treffen hier meist beim Sonnenaufgang ein. Die Ursache hierfuer ist, dass der Verkehr hier bei Tageslicht nur statt findet, da das Zoll - Haus so wie saemmtliche Bureaus beim Sonnen Untergang geschlossen zu werden pflegen. Schon von weiten sieht der ankommende Seefahrer den im Morgengrau gehuellten hohen Libanon, auf dem im Winter bis tief hinab der Schnee lagert.

Unser Schiff faengt schon an die Fahrt zu verlangsamen, da wir uns der Hafen-einfahrt naehern. Oh, welch entzueckenden Anblick bietet uns jetzt die Aussicht ueber die freundliche Stadt, ueber Berg und Tal! Man kann sich in der Tat kaum genug sehen. Ein kleiner Schlappdampfer kommte entgegen gefahren um das ankommende Schiff langsam in den inneren Hafen hinein zu buchsieren. Im Hafen angelangt, erblickt man unzaehlige Ruderboete, deren Sitzplaetze mit huebschen orientalischen Teppichen bedeckt sind u nd im ganzen sehr sauber aussehen. Jedes von diesen Boeten will das Erste an der Schiffstreppe sein, doch darf sich keines derselben naehern, bis der Schiffsartzt, der an Land gefahren ist, um die tuerkische Behoerde ueber den Gesundheitszustand an Bord zu berichten die Erlaubniss zur Ausschiffung eingeholt hat. Sobald nun dieser mit der sogennanten

First typewritten version of Sayyida Salme's manuscript

Syrische Sitten und Gebräuche.

Die Stadt Beyrut liegt sehr malerisch hingestreckt; umgeben von dem hohen Libanon und bespült vom mittelländischen Meer macht sie auf den Ankömmling einen höchst angenehmen Eindruck. Die von Norden oder Süden kommenden Schiffe treffen hier meist beim Sonnenaufgang ein. Die Ursache hier ist, dass der Verkehr hier nur bei Tageslicht stattfindet, da das Zollhaus sowie sämtliche Bureaux beim Sonnenuntergang geschlossen zu werden pflegen. Schon von weitem sieht der ankommende Seefahrer den im Morgengrau gehüllten hohen Libanon, auf dem im Winter bis tief hinab der Schnee lagert.

Unser Schiff fängt schon an die Fahrt zu verlangsamen, da wir uns der Hafeneinfahrt nähern. Oh, welch entzückenden Anblick bietet uns jetzt die Aussicht über die freundliche Stadt, über Berg und Tal : Man kann sich in der Tat kaum satt sehen. Ein kleiner Schleppdampfer kommt uns entgegen gefahren, um das ankommende Schiff langsam in den inneren Hafen hinein zu bugsieren. Im Hafen angelangt, erblickt man unzählige Ruderboote, deren Sitzplätze mit hübschen orientalischen Teppichen bedeckt sind und im ganzen sehr sauber aussehen. Jedes von diesen Booten will das erste an der Schiffstreppe sein, doch darf sich keines derselben nähern, bis der Schiffsarzt, der an Land gefahren ist, um die türkische Behörde über den Gesundheitszustand an Bord zu berichten, die Erlaubnis zur Ausschiffung eingeholt hat. Sobald nun dieser mit der sogenannten prattica zurückkommt, strömen die Insassen der kleinen Ruderboote an Bord des Schiffes, um sich der

Second typewritten version of Sayyida Salme's manuscript

Syrian Customs and Conventions

The city of Beirut has a most picturesque layout. Surrounded by the highlands of Lebanon and bathed by the Mediterranean Sea, it makes a most pleasant first impression on visitors. Ships coming from the North or South usually arrive as the sun rises. It is a fact that traffic here happens only during the daytime, since the customs building, and all the various offices, are wont to close by sunset. Arriving sailors can see the Lebanese heights already from afar, shrouded in the fog of dawn, and in the winter covered deep down the slopes with snow.

Our ship is already starting to slow down, as we near the entrance to the harbor. Oh, what a lovely sight lies before us, across the welcoming city, across mountains and valley! There is, in point of fact, no getting one's fill from this view. A small tugboat approaches us to tow the arriving ship slowly into the inner port. Once in the port, the sight is full of countless rowboats, whose seats are covered with beautiful Oriental rugs and look very clean overall. Every one of these boats wants to be first in line at the ship's stairs, and yet none may come near until the ship's doctor, who has traveled to shore to report on the health conditions on board, has received permission from the Turkish authorities to disembark. As soon as this doctor returns with the so-called *prattica*, the occupants of these little rowboats swarm on board the ship to confirm their passengers, or to pick up friends or acquaintances. Whoever is lucky enough to be picked up by friends or acquaintances can be glad to avoid various inconveniences, particularly if the native tongue—in this case, Arabic—is unfamiliar. Usually there are many, mostly very clean carriages, almost all of which are Victorias, standing in front of the customs house that one has to pass through, ready to pick up any foreigners.

The streets of Beirut even on the outskirts of the city are mostly wide, but very poorly maintained, as the honorable municipality prefers to let the communal taxes disappear into its own pockets, instead of, as it should be, using them for the benefit of the community. And therefore, the summer dust and winter mire are permanent guests on the streets. As soon as one steps into one of the invariably very airy and massively built houses, those dirty streets that were just traversed are quickly forgotten.

/Everything here is nice and neat, even in the very poorest homes. The finer houses are completely laid out with marble floors; polished red tiles are now and again selected for the bedrooms. The manner of constructing houses is very simple, but suited to the climate and very comfortable. One usually enters directly into a very large hallway, completely covered with marble and about eleven meters long and seven meters wide. From there, any number of doors lead into rooms on the east, south, and west. A high window and a door that opens onto a balcony finish off the house on the north. This northern-facing room usually serves as the living room and stays cool throughout the summer, since it has no direct exposure to the sun. The best rooms in the house lie in the west, from whence a refreshing breeze is usually blowing, which makes these rooms particularly well-suited for bedrooms.

Beirut has a water pipeline, as well as gas lighting. The water travels down from Lebanon and is simply unmatched in quality. The fact that Beirut has seldom experienced a harmful epidemic is attributed to the good characteristics of the water. There were times when cholera was spreading in Egypt, Jaffa, Damascus, and neighboring Tripoli, while Beirut was completely spared. Food and rent is very cheap here; one can see that the people—by which I naturally mean the local population—are well-nourished.

The Residents

Syrians consistently come across as very intelligent. Their faces and figures are attractive; the coal-black eyes, and also the hair, notably of the youth, but above all of the women, may be called very beautiful. The men possess undeniable business skills worth marveling at; they are all, so-to-speak, born businessmen. With demonstrative talent in making money, even very simple folk often become rich so quickly that they are soon multi-millionaires (calculated in Franks). They love to imitate all things European, which frequently does them no favors, especially in their attire, as, for example, with their handsome head coverings. Their red fez looks much better on them than the European hats.

One particular major evil passion rules the population, namely the harmful game of hazard.[50] Rich people are said to play uninterrupted all day and night, whether in the club or their own homes. When they have trouble finding a partner, they entice their cooks, servants, or coachmen to play until someone else fills in. This passion has also taken hold of the women, who in this respect concede little to their men. Of course, there are also many exceptions, who strongly denounce their fellow citizens.

The population here is divided into two groups: Muslim and Christian. Although the first are fewer in number, they dominate to a much greater extent. Not because the state government is Muslim, but because the weaker group receives more government protection. This is generally how Turkish rule operates;[51] the weaker ones get more protection than the stronger ones. Whether Christian or Muslim, it is the same, as evidenced by the situation in Jaffa. There the Christians are in the minority and find consideration in every respect, as acknowledged by those affected. These state politics have, however, had a somewhat dispiriting effect on the Christian population in Beirut, despite it being in the majority over other religions. Accordingly, these Christians are also, as is commonly known, not exactly heroes. But in their defense, there is the fact that they, as Christians, are never drafted into the military and thus never get to experience the tough and very disciplined life in the service.

Foreigners are somewhat taken aback to discover that Syrians have practically no patriotic feelings! Syrians just want to know that the country is in the hands of one of the great European powers, according to their liking, of course, ideally with either England or France as their ruler. Beyond that, they have no shortage of personal pride. Both adults and adolescents possess sufficient self-esteem.

There are also many Jews who pursue their livelihoods as workers or merchants. They can mostly be seen on Saturday afternoons, with the women

---

50 A two-dice betting game that dates back to the Middle Ages, often likened to craps.
51 Syria was part of the Ottoman Empire and was governed by Turkish rulers until the Empire's collapse in 1918.

Syrian Customs and Conventions

and girls looking their finest, as they walk in droves on the beach. The devout women in the group wear wigs or headscarves, still very much in the old style. By contrast, the young generation is in very modern dress. Since only those who believe in the Mohammedan religion are drafted into the military, all other believers are free of the draft.

Syrians are very hospitable, and the more guests to care for, the happier they are. In conversation, they often address total strangers with "oh, my uncle" or "oh, my aunt," which sounds rather droll. Even small children are often referred to this way. In general, their behavior is very courteous, and they are polite beyond reproach. The one thing where they go a bit overboard is in the many compliments they make, even though they are truly masterful in this. Their character cannot always be described as open, and they are a bit veiled, for they are quite skilled in concealing their true opinion behind a deluge of meaningless words. Whenever they wish to skirt a question that might not be all that comfortable, they respond with a counterquestion to circumvent the answer.

What distinguishes Syrians, in their favor, from so many other cultures is their love of cleanliness. Even the simplest folk put great stock in keeping things clean, which makes a very favorable impression.

The well-to-do folk live totally *à la franca*, which is to say, according to European custom. They eat with knives and forks at set tables, sleep on European beds, and use whatever is needed for their comfort. This makes for great contrasts in that these same people, who are often surrounded by every conceivable convenience, also frequently have parents, siblings, and near relations that still live the way it was done a thousand years before, with no sense at all for using beds or table settings. It appears quite odd when a Syrian lady, dressed in the absolute latest Paris fashion from head to foot, rushes by in her equipage, while the mother or aunt sits beside her still wearing her traditional attire, with a black, silken mantilla on her head, rather than an imposing Parisian hat. The same applies to modern gentlemen, who sport European hats, while their relatives have kept the old headdress.

/The contrasts between the old and new generations can often have a strange effect on observers. There they are, the honorable old men, sitting on their divan, drinking black coffee, and smoking their *nargile* (hookah pipe), as in time immemorial, mindful and thoughtful, while their offspring sit beside them on modern, European seating, dressed in the latest Parisian look and speaking French amongst themselves. The latter is spoken as fine and accent-free as possible. Indeed, on the subject of learning foreign languages, the Syrians are masterfully predisposed. People who speak four or six foreign languages are not unusual. This race is very intelligent, very teachable, and hard working.

/As an example: There are a great number of wholesale merchants, bankers, and commissioners who work primarily with Europeans and who take their rising sons directly from school into their own shops to teach them on the spot. These inexperienced, half-grown boys are then soon so skilled in their trade that they quickly become the mainstay of their fathers. The people also possess a most astonishing ability to grasp things. A seamstress, for example, who can neither read nor write, nor even owns the otherwise indispensable measuring tape, sits on a mat on the floor and, following a picture she has been shown in a fashion magazine, produces the very finest high society and ball outfits.

Antonie's 1898 wedding in the Hotel Bassoul in Beirut

Sayyida Salme standing in the front yard of her 1909 Beirut home

At the front entrance of the same home, from Rudolph's album

From Rudolph's album, Sayyida Salme's first residence in Beirut

Ground floor, Sayyida Salme's daughter Rosa seated on the right

ON FAITH

There is no way to understand Sayyida Salme's life without considering her faith—by probing both her own beliefs and the religions that framed them.[52] Faith was her ultimate touchstone and throughline. Sayyida Salme's connection to God is the backdrop to all of her writings, as is the impact of religious dictates on her life. Throughout her formative years in Zanzibar and her transformative years in Germany, faith posed a duality that was profoundly personal and excruciatingly public. It embodied her spiritual connection as a social construct in ways that both stabilized and destabilized her.

Who am I to speak about her faith? Spiritual beliefs are intensely personal. I hold this question of faith in my hand—pen poised—and hardly dare go there. But there is plenty to say, even beyond the many things she said herself, about this—what is the word?—penumbra, essence, omnipresence—by which she defined her world, which in turn defined her. This essay can do no more than tap at the edges, knowing the topic is broader and deeper than any pen can consider. What faith meant to her can only be answered by what she said and believed. In writing this essay, my thoughts are but a distant prism to refract some light onto her life and writings.

Sayyida Salme had three principal phases in her life, with three geographies that also framed her faith: Zanzibar where she grew up as a Muslim until the age of twenty-two; Germany where she lived as a Christian until the age of forty-four; and the Middle East, principally Beirut, where she found her liminal space and stayed until the age of seventy.[53] Her pivot from Zanzibar to Germany came when she fell in love with a German merchant, Heinrich Ruete, and chose him as her husband. It was a choice that cascaded her into much lack of choice, including her conversion to Christianity.

In this long life of almost eighty years, there is one compelling truth: Faith was the source of both her anguish and relief. It tied her to her homeland in the

---

52 At the outset, it is important to note the difference between faith and religion. In simple terms, faith comes from the inside, religion from the outside. At the nexus, faith is the translation of an established belief system into personal beliefs. It is also the connection of personal beliefs into a community of practice.
53 See my first blog entry, "The Liminal In-Between," at www.sayyidasalme.com/blog. Her last ten years were spent back in Germany with her youngest daughter, until she died in Jena on February 29, 1924.

East and unsettled her when she moved to the West. It divided her into the before and after, here and there. Faith came from her core, as her source of meaning and purpose in life, but was shaped by others, by religious mores, rules, laws, the Koran and the Bible, as directed by authorities and society—with a violence that cut her to the core.

No bloodied Omani khanjar split her skin, and yet her conversion did no less damage when it dissected her soul. Like an amputation, the cut left her exposed and flailing:

> Divorced from my old beliefs, and attached to the new in name only, I began a time for which I have no words. Never in my whole life—neither before nor after—did I feel so morally bereft, robbed of every support, as right after my baptism. . . . [T]here is no doubt that it is a thousand times better to be a Muslim than to be neither Christian (meaning from the heart) nor Muslim. And it was with this largest possible chasm inside me that I entered Europe and its hallowed civilization. I fought internally with myself, no one surmising how much I suffered in silence. Not even to my own beloved husband could I openly admit that our views differed on this point. (*Letters*, pp. 8–9)

To add to this agony, can anyone even imagine what she felt when—literally days later—her infant son, whose budding life in her womb had precipitated her escape, died on the train as they travelled between Lyon and Paris on the way to Hamburg? What she thought of herself, and what she thought the Lord was saying to her, we will never know, as she never wrote a single word about it.

In time, she found some healing, but the scars barely masked the inner conflict. As she confronted one obstacle after another, and life descended into poverty, her distress continued to echo in the void. "Soon I also came to see the power of religion as the most powerful of all when it comes to affecting our inner lives and well-being." (*Letters*, p. 9) "Spiritual emptiness and loneliness, plus the early darkness of the winter days, conspired to oppress me." (*Letters*, p. 64)

Yet, where religion cleft her asunder, she managed to find footing in her underlying faith. To take one example, the first time she was in a German church, she still felt her God:

> Having taken my place on a pew between other congregants, I was overcome with an indescribable feeling of trepidation, which continued to worsen as I realized that the church service kept on going. I naturally could not understand a word of what was being sung and said. But the

sense that I was in the holiest sanctuary soon calmed me. (*Letters*, p. 32) Later [after Heinrich's death], it was indeed a great comfort for me to have been together with him in church shortly before his accident. For even though I had barely understood the sermon, simply the thought of being in the Lord's house has always given me fulfillment and kept me from becoming discouraged. (*Letters*, p. 50)

And again, after she learned of her brother Sultan Madjid's death: "Only my old trust in the Almighty held me upright and kept my courage, at that moment, from sinking all too much." (*Letters*, p. 60)

With this enduring devotion to God, it is tempting to suggest that the difference between Islam and Christianity did not need to create such a chasm in Sayyida Salme's life. It was, after all, the same Abrahamic God.[54] In those last months in Zanzibar, perhaps she had a naïve sense that crossing over to Christianity would be eased by this continuity. Or maybe, looking up to her husband, looking up to the West, she might have trusted that the "enlightened" ways held great promise. Then again, maybe she just trusted herself to find her way, as she had all along. For what did she know about the brave new world she was about to enter, or any world beyond her limited confines? She surely had no inkling of how little would carry over, how disappointed, even despairing, she would become. Realistically, she probably had no real room or means to think about it at all.

Whatever the case, it was all irrelevant once she chose her husband—and let me put "chose" in quotes, since we may fall in love more than we scan and select. Occam's Razor would point us to the simplest truth: Love conquers all. After that, there was no further choice in the matter. Conversion was the step she had to take.

We can thus trace her transgressive choice of husband to the severe consequences that followed. A Christian husband meant a Christian marriage, which for her meant a Christian baptism, both of which took place back-to-back in Aden on the very same day—May 30, 1867—only shortly after she saw Heinrich for the first time in nine months since fleeing the island and first introduced him to their infant son. This was the day her identity changed from princess in the royal family to wife of a German merchant, when her name changed from Sayyida Salme to Emily Ruete. It was also the day they left for Europe, when she was catapulted from East to West across a newly risen wall of religion that stood as a boundary with no way back.

---

54 Muslims view Jews and Christians as "people of the book," reflecting a recognition of shared early scripts and a shared, monotheistic belief in but one, true God.

Emily's baptism recorded on the Archdeaconry and Diocese of Bombay's form

To be clear, her conversion was the issue, the gravest sin under *Sharia* Islamic law, not her contact with a German man, nor even the pregnancy, though those were bad enough. It was the rejection of Islam that was considered inexcusable. No matter that she did not reject religion altogether, but stayed fully committed to a belief in God. No matter that the conversion was not a choice per se, just a pre-condition for her marriage. Devout as she was, she might well have stayed Muslim, had that been allowed. But no, Christianity was her only option. And this was the travesty, the treason. Death, or at the very least imprisonment, was at the time—and in some cases remains today—the expected punishment for voluntary rejection of Islam.

It is plausible that the Ibadi Islam of the Omani Sultanate, with its tradition of moderation and tolerance, might have put less emphasis on official retribution, and instead put the onus on the defector's accountability to God, but no one gave Sayyida Salme a free pass. When word came around that she would be "sent to Mecca"[55]—and everyone knew what that meant—it was a clear invitation for her to leave the island. Whether she chose to do so of her own free will may still be debated. Yes, there should be no doubt that she chose her

---

55 Said to be "tantamount to a death sentence." E. van Donzel, p. 14.

husband,[56] but did all the sequelae of her need to flee the island and her need to answer "yes" to the pastor[57] meet the criterion that she voluntarily rejected Islam, as Islamic doctrine requires? [58] On that August evening as she set foot in the Indian Ocean, and on that May day in Aden when she took her Christian name, how voluntary was it?

We hear her cry for help as they left Marseille, headed for Hamburg:

> As we drove from our hotel to the train station, I was gripped by such an unfamiliar fear that I would have preferred to scream out loud. I had the feeling as though, from this moment on, my homeland was being pulled ever further from me, and all the bridges were crashing in behind me. The cry of my soul for you turned into a thousand voices from my beloved island, all seemingly calling to me in unison: "Do not go any further, better to return again!" I fought a terrible fight within myself. Like an automaton, I stepped into the train that would now seek to take me, as quickly as possible, to an unknown land, to total strangers, as if I was in the greatest hurry to reach my future destination. And so we kept on riding toward the North. (*Letters*, p. 6)

For most of us today, the consequences of choosing our partners, married or not, are nowhere near as stark. In Sayyida Salme's time and place, however, this was a hard border, an either/or and no in-between. In choosing Heinrich, she lost almost everything—her homeland, family, close friends, possessions, properties, and past; everything familiar was brutally wrenched from her. And when even her religion was exchanged, she lost an integral piece of herself that was replaced by something that at first meant nothing. The only foothold she had left was in herself, in Heinrich, and in what she could make of her faith.

Years later, she asked herself the question: "I left my homeland as a complete Arab and a good Muslim, and what am I today?" (*Memoirs*, p. 217) She then responded: "A poor Christian and somewhat more than half a German." It is a favorite and oft-cited quote. Yet, what typical readers of the *Memoirs* do not know is that she later struck that answer when she marked up her *Memoiren* for

---

56 See the excerpt from her son Rudolph's letter that I describe in my essay "On Freedom." (*Letters*, p. 130)
57 See my footnote on her affirmation in English. (*Letters*, footnote 34, p.8)
58 Notably, traditional Islam did not support forced conversions. Modern interpretations go further and accept freedom of belief in quoting from the Koran that "there is no compulsion in religion." (Surah Al-Baqarah 2:256)

subsequent publication.[59] It speaks volumes that she originally responded as she did, but it speaks even more loudly that she then crossed it out. It tells us that, over time, she became more certain of her Christianity and claimed it for her own. We do her wrong to tether her to an unevolving sense of her own spirituality.

The early years were, however, no less agonizing. The problem was not just the switch from one religion to another, but also the straddle that left her hanging between religions, not knowing what to make of herself or the new religion. Worse than being neither-nor was being a fraud. It was a condition that plagued her from page to page:

> On top of that, to be called Christian, even though I was as much a Muslim inside as you yourself. Through and through, I felt so despicable that I should appear different from what I actually was. I will tell you this in unvarnished frankness: Beware of changing your religion without complete conviction! Conviction? Yes, from whom and what should I have gained any conviction? No one, as it was, cared one whit about my true faith. . . . I felt so despicably false to be considered a Christian when I had absolutely no clear idea *how and what* Christianity even means. (*Letters*, pp. 8–9)

> The thought that kept me so preoccupied put my poor soul into great conflict. I found so few good examples of devout Christians that I personally felt I was neither fish nor fowl. Separated from my former beliefs, I had nonetheless found no real replacement. How was I, as a Mohammedan, supposed to feel attracted to the new faith, when even the people who were born and bred Christian were so disdainful toward their own religion? Your kind heart would certainly have suffered, had you been able to see into my tormented soul. (*Letters*, pp. 26–27)

> [I]t became quite clear to me that being Christian was a relative term. Accordingly, my inner struggle grew more and more excruciating every day. (*Letters*, p. 36)

Her spirituality was terribly unsettled in those early years. It was an immense struggle to find herself and her God within the religions that defined him. Understandably, she kept reverting back to the God of her childhood when

---

[59] Although there was no subsequent publication—the family was apparently unable to find a willing publisher—her intention to delete is clear. My new *Memoirs* translation incorporates all her edits from her hand-marked edition, found in the Leiden University Libraries Special Collections at NINO SR 613 a-b. For more on this, see my essay "On Translating" in the *Memoirs* (specifically p. 254).

Christianity failed to replace the ingrained rituals and threatened to strain the relationship between her and the Almighty. As she wrote to her counterpart in Zanzibar: "To console you, I can also let you know that, in the initial years after my baptism, I instinctively recited my old prayer to myself whenever I was alone" (*Letters*, p. 9)—all the while consoling herself.

If we consider the essential differences between Islam and Christianity, doctrinally and practically, it seems that Sayyida Salme's upbringing persisted beyond her Christian conversion. Even after she gave herself up to her new religion, her reliance on an undifferentiated God appears to continue. There is no sense of the trinity. We never hear her address Christ or Jesus, the son of God, directly. Instead, her account of the early years in Germany is filled with appeals only to God, the Lord. "Have I not, in my difficult position, unceasingly asked the dear God for help and support, since I always remained discontented inside, indeed utterly miserable." (*Letters*, p. 69)

For Sayyida Salme, it seems that God the Almighty was still the maker and mover of all.[60] There is but one moment after her husband's death when she lost that certainty and could not pray—"I felt spurned by my Creator and was thus totally unmoored"—until she finally caught herself again in the prayer of her youth: "Nothing shall ever happen to us but what the Lord has decreed for us, so praise be unto him forever, Amen!" (*Letters*, p. 55) And yet, she knew that this Islamic belief in destiny did not translate well into Christianity. She seems to have held back on her views to others, so as not to come across as ignorant, or humiliate herself, or discover what she did not want to know.[61] But in a telling passage, we hear her resisting with reproof:

> Certainly, now and again there were people who meant well with me and tried to comfort me in their way. I say, in their way, because after I once called out in utter despair: "Oh, if I knew not that this was

---

[60] This reflected the Islam in which she was raised: "A Muslim not only recognizes his God as his creator and keeper, but also feels the presence of the Lord at all times. He is certain that it is not his will, but the will of the Lord that comes to pass, in all things, large and small." (*Memoirs*, p. 14)

[61] She was, for example, "acutely interested" in her first Christmas experience, "not having wanted to ask my husband about [Christian festivals]—on the one hand, out of consideration for his feelings toward his religion (for what did I know back then of the countless ways to profess one's Christianity?), and on the other hand—and that was the main thing for me—to avoid discovering that the Christian religion was in fact, as some tended to believe in our parts, idol worship. Exactly that would have been contrary to my convictions. For these reasons, I steered clear of any questions pertaining to the upcoming celebration." (*Letters*, pp. 34–35)

my God's will, I could never find peace!", the response was to try to reeducate me. I was asked if I really believed that God in fact takes care of our fates and everything we encounter on this earth. I need not describe to you how innerly appalled I was at this profane question. It seems to me that but a very few, select Christians are familiar with the complete Holy Scripture, which clearly enough tells us that the Lord knows the number of our hairs and that no sparrow falls off the roof without His will. On such occasions, I could not thank the Lord enough for letting me enter this world as a Muslim. (*Letters*, pp. 64–65)

As she describes in the *Memoirs*, her life growing up in Zanzibar had few distractions and even fewer obligations. She had time and space to amply live out her faith, not only to pray five times a day, but also to register virtually every act from a faith-based perspective. This was in the nature of the Muslim experience, where social rituals are particularly pronounced, where religion is often described as a lifestyle. Indeed, the *Memoirs* offer a rare ethnological insight into the totality of the Muslim experience in the harem and royal household. It is an excellent primer on how Islam's code of conduct structured all hours of the day, especially in the absence of other structure. As Sayyida Salme says: "In our house, with its hundreds of residents, fixed rules were elusive, since everyone could and did follow their own tastes and convenience. Only the two main meals and regularly recurring prayers forced the community to live according to a specific, more established order." The ensuing pages lay out the course of the full day. (*Memoirs*, pp. 39-42) It is no surprise then, when she gets to describing her later life in Germany, that the *Letters* painfully witness Sayyida Salme's grasping search for a Christian equivalent.

The shock of switching religions also came with the overwhelming inundation of everything new and incredible, often incomprehensible, in the West. In effect, Sayyida Salme moved from a life where her faith could be central and practical to a life where it was intangible and elusive. Rather than living a religion that was patterned into the daily rituals, her European communing with God was all but crowded out—first, by all the new, but even over time, by a much busier life, especially as a bereft, impoverished widow with three small children. Is this a fair statement: Her reaching for God took far more effort and extra intention right at the time when she needed him most? She does not talk about it this way, but this crowding out feels palpable. With her change in setting, her changed lifestyle became more existential than spiritual. And yet, the spiritual remained as existential as ever to who she was.

Not for lack of trying, it was all about the struggle. Poor Christian and half a German? We can ask ourselves why Sayyida Salme chose to delete those words, but the rest of her words tell us that they were, in any case, too simplistic, too categorical a description for what she was made to endure. Arab society, however—at least the patriarchal dynasty—saw none of the nuance and refused to forgive. It left no room for any residual attachment or deeper connection. In an instant, she was reduced to an insurmountable label: infidel, apostate, heretic. All else, it seemed, might somehow be absolved, but not her rejection of Islam.

———·•·———

Why was her conversion so threatening to society that it merited death? That she would be so dangerous as to be disappeared? Was it about religion, sex, purity of the blood line, social cohesion, all of the above? It did not help that Sayyida Salme was subjecting herself to an encroaching colonial power, an abandonment of Islam with greater political bite. It also did not help that she was a princess, not just anyone, but representative of the royal house. Failure to rein her in would make the Sultan look weak, no matter how sympathetic he might have been to her cause.[62]

From a modern lens, it seems apparent that this was also about guarding and controlling women. In the hierarchy of the patriarchy, it was acceptable for Muslim men to marry non-Muslims, notably Christian and Jewish women "of the book"[63]—but not the other way around. Why? Because it was assumed that men would be in charge of the home. Wives would presumably accept the husband's religion, but whether converted or not, the main point was the fate of the children. If the man was in charge, the children would be raised under Islam. Socially speaking, it seems, men's eyes could roam as long as Islam ruled the home. By contrast, Islam typically considered matrimony between a Muslim woman and a Christian man invalid. Not only was the marriage rejected, but social rejection would follow as well.[64]

In Germany, too, interfaith marriage was frowned upon, if not forbidden. In this specific case, Heinrich was a Lutheran from the outwardly positioned,

---

62 Her half-brother Madjid, who was Sultan at the time she fled, was indeed very supportive of his errant half-sister, even after she participated in the coup against him. The two had reconciled before she left the island, and it is clear that he wished her no harm. (*Memoirs*, pp. 201–3)
63 See footnote 54 above.
64 In the Arab world, gender differences around marriage are still remarkably pronounced today. See, for example, "An Insta Triple Talaq" on my blog at www.sayyidasalme.com/blog. From speaking to Omani women, I hear that social pressures also keep women constrained even where rules and laws have changed, perhaps even more than in Sayyida Salme's time. Comparisons can be made with her chapters "Arab Matrimony" and "Arab Visits Among the Ladies." (*Memoirs*, pp. 123–32)

trade-oriented port city of Hamburg. But even though Protestants were less rigid than Catholics, and even though this autonomous city-state was more cosmopolitan than other parts of Germany, social codes and proper behavior in Sayyida Salme's new setting left little room for exotic entanglements.

To be sure, Sayyida Salme's conversion was both a religious betrayal and a social violation. This is even evident in the institutional response. In Sayyida Salme's case, it apparently did not matter that both Christianity and Islam were happy to gain new believers. Christianity preaches conversion as a pathway to salvation, and Muslims believe in the universality of Islam; both are called to bring others into their religious folds for the betterment of humanity. In all its missionary zeal of the time, including in East Africa, did the Protestant church appreciate that Sayyida Salme had found her way to Jesus? Did it at least recognize and nurture her intense effort to crack the code of Christianity? Not that the record shows. The brunt that she bore for leaving Islam, it seems, was not compensated by much of any affirmation by the Christian church. It may not be farfetched to think that many Christians could not see past her Oriental exoticism to embrace Sayyida Salme as one of them.[65]

Notably, the couple was not married in either Zanzibar or Germany. They could not wed in Zanzibar, where the union was out of the question,[66] and they could not travel and arrive respectably in Hamburg as a couple with a child without already being married. Instead, they tied the knot in Aden, apparently another one of those liminal spaces, in the Anglican Christ Church[67] with an English minister.[68] And that had its consequences, too. This riveting act of mixed-faith, mixed-race matrimony not only cost Sayyida Salme her religious and royal identities, but, unbeknownst to Heinrich, also cost him his national identity. Only later did he discover that he was no longer a citizen of Hamburg—he had apparently become stateless. Fortunately for him, he was

---

[65] This was also the time that Christian missionaries in East Africa engaged in mass conversions to bring enlightenment and salvation to local "primitives"; academic endeavors to document "scientific racism" were flourishing; and the gawking public was drawn in masses to popular human zoos, which started, of all places, in Hamburg. See my blog post "Who remembers human zoos?" at www.sayyidasalme.com/blog.

[66] As Sayyida Salme herself succinctly says: "A union with my beloved would have been impossible in my homeland, so I naturally harbored the wish to leave the island quietly." (*Memoirs*, p. 202)

[67] See G.S.P. Freeman-Grenville's annotated reprint of the 1888 Ward & Downey *Memoirs of an Arabian Princess*, p. 319 (1981) (hereinafter G.S.P. Freeman-Grenville).

[68] "My baptism took place in the English chapel in Aden . . . Immediately after that, our wedding took place according to English rituals." (*Memoirs*, p. 202) Notably, when preparing her marked copy for re-publication, Sayyida Salme deleted the accompanying statement that she had received prior religious instruction.

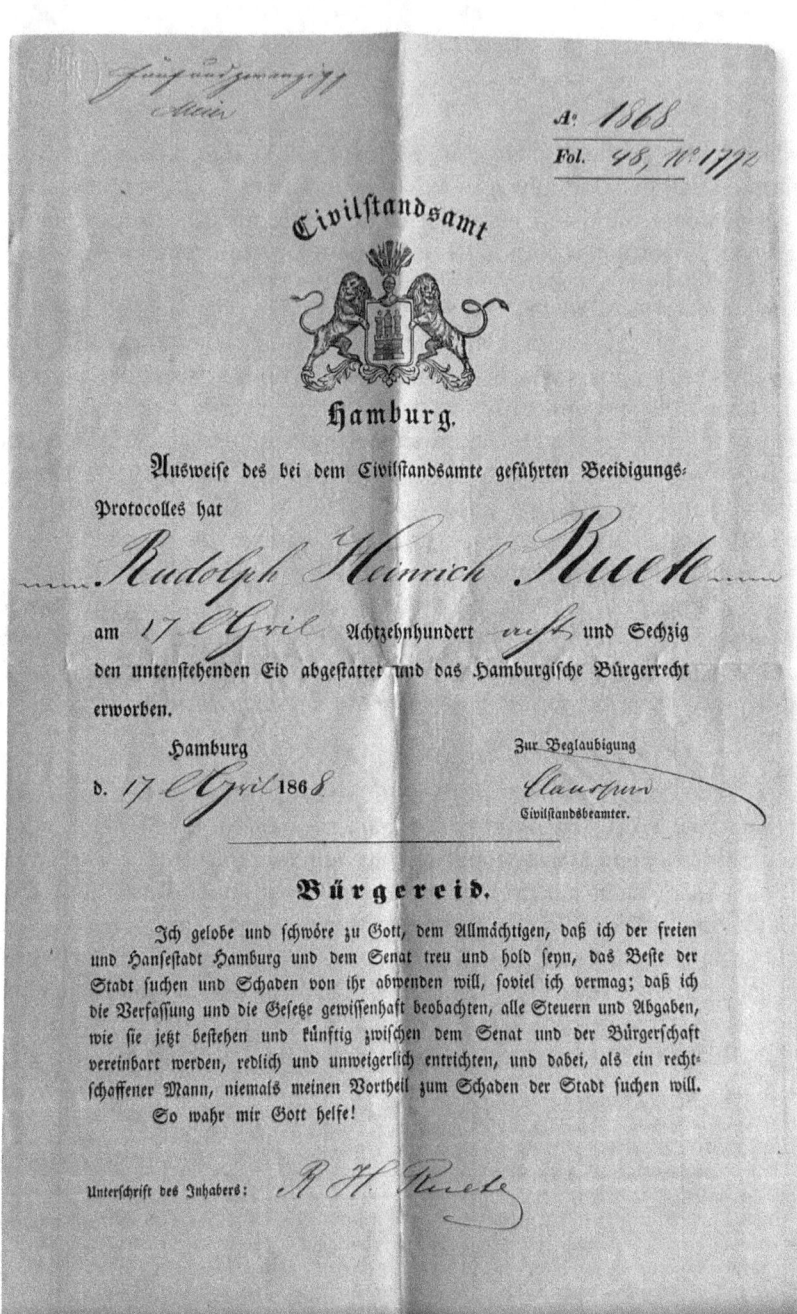

Rudolph Heinrich Ruete's oath of citizenship from 1868

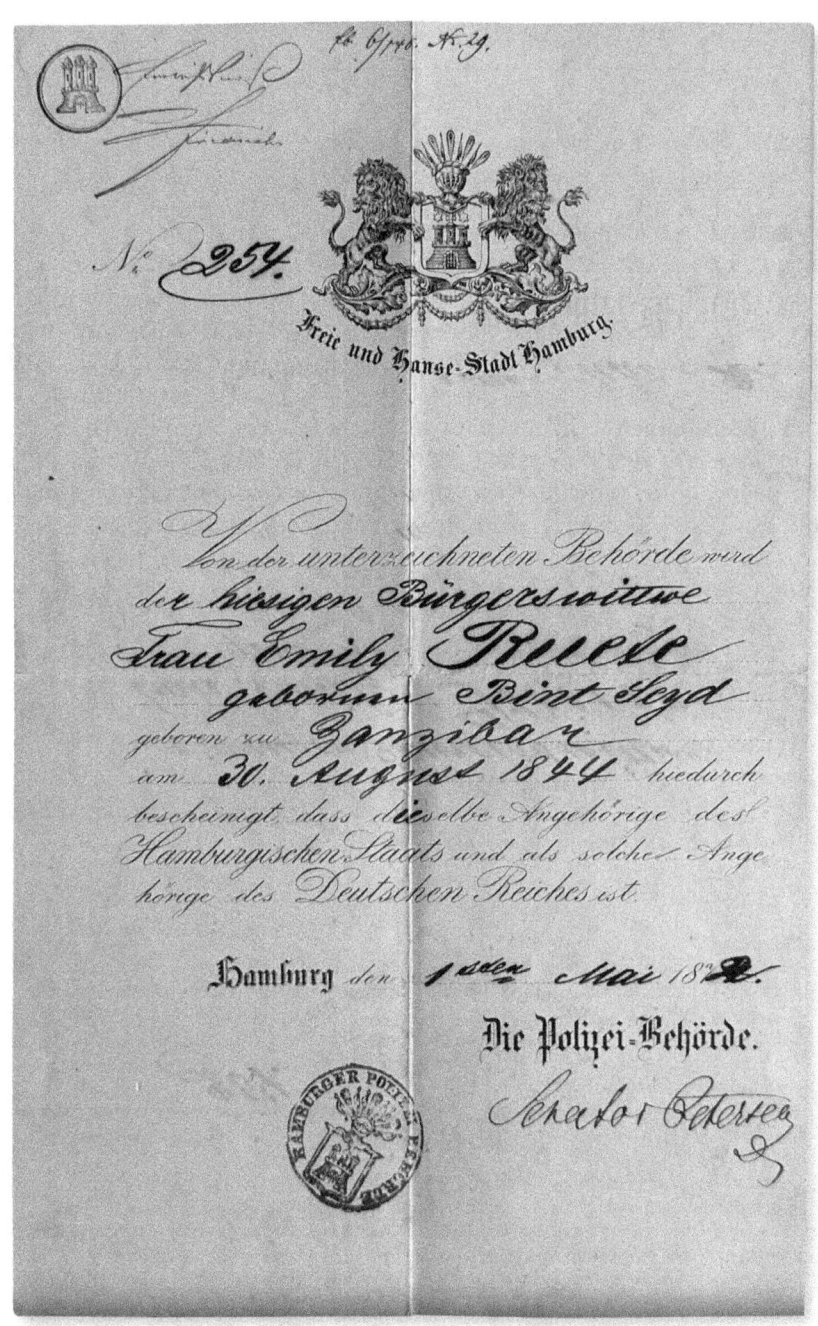

Emily Ruete's certification of citizenship from 1872

quickly able to regain his status.[69] Sayyida Salme, in turn, became a citizen of Hamburg as a widow some years later.[70]

This unforeseen loss of citizenship was not a fluke, but the norm. It reflected geopolitical attitudes at a time when dual loyalty and dual citizenship were not recognized. The act of marrying abroad essentially meant subjecting oneself to another country's regime, thereby signaling diminished loyalty to the state. In this respect, Sayyida Salme's conversion from Islam to Christianity also mapped onto the larger Oriental-Occidental divide, in which religious identity was largely conflated with social and national identity. The choice of Islam or Christianity was not just a religious marker, but also a cultural and political one, through which boundaries were set and on which public cohesion rested. Crossover marriages not only bucked the established order, but also threatened political primacy, particularly at a time when Muslim societies were loath to give any further influence and dominance to Western colonial powers.

At some level, lighter touchpoints through trade and exploration were fine,[71] even crossovers through slavery and *sarari* (concubines) were fine, but losing a princess to a foreign marriage was not. With stability resting on East-West divisions, the different religions played their parts in creating recognizable borders. That Sayyida Salme was seen by the British as a wild card that could undermine their cunning diplomacy,[72] that her status as a German citizen was

---

69 We know this from records that Fridjof Gutendorf found deep in the Hamburg archives—our thanks to him for his extensive efforts. As the records show, a proverbially diligent bureaucrat came across the discrepancy when handling the birth certificate of Antonie, the couple's first child born in Hamburg. Issuance of the birth certificate was delayed until the matter was resolved. Since Heinrich came from a well-established, upstanding family, the whole procedure, from application to Hamburg Senate confirmation, took little more than a week.
70 At the same time, Sayyida Salme acquired German citizenship as an automatic add-on, following German unification in 1871. It is an odd history that Heinrich, who died in 1870, never became a German citizen, while his Omani/Zanzibari wife did.
71 Indeed, it was basically business as usual when Heinrich was allowed to continue his commercial activities in Zanzibar without restraint or repercussion in the months after the scandal became known.
72 As part of her "education" in the West, Sayyida Salme eventually became wise to the games that countries play: "Later, I came to better understand why my deeply desired reconciliation with my brother would have been especially unwelcome in London at that very moment. Since the Sultan neither speaks a European language, nor understands the subtleties of European diplomacy, the English wanted to keep him in a complete state of ignorance to ensure no last-minute trouble in getting specific treaties signed. Had I in fact made peace with him, they assumed I would have used my somewhat broader knowledge of European affairs to share various bits of information that would have benefited him and Zanzibar, but been all the more contrary to English government interests. Without suspecting a thing, I had simply become a victim of these 'humane' politics." (*Memoirs*, p. 210)

later put into play against her Sultan brother Barghash,[73] and that she herself confidentially wrote to Sultan Barghash that she could "be useful to you with all the arts of Europe,"[74] went straight to the point.

The controversy around Sayyida Salme's conversion also signaled the primacy of the church. Even though her father had dropped the Imam part of his title, preferring to use only Sayyid as the Omani equivalent for Sultan,[75] he was the picture of piety, signaling to the Omani and Zanzibari people over which he ruled that Allah ruled above all. There was no discernible daylight between his reign and his religion. Sayyid Madjid, who succeeded his father, was also entirely devout, and the subsequent Sayyid Barghash even more so. Barghash, feeling justified by her travesty against the Almighty, persisted to his dying day with his refusal to reconcile, claiming "I have no sister, she died many years ago."[76]

In Germany, on the other hand, a little daylight between church and state appeared with the dawn of the *Kulturkampf* (literally translated "culture war") under Chancellor Otto von Bismarck. It is a quirk of fate that the German Civil Marriage Act[77] was passed only a few years after Sayyida Salme found the love of her life. Until then, marriage had been entirely controlled by the church, but suddenly the state was stepping in. As of 1875, German marriages could be officially recognized only through administrative acts, which had to happen first. This opened the door to unions outside of Catholicism and Protestantism, at least theoretically. Surprising as it may be, a Hamburg administrator could have legally married a Christian Heinrich and a Muslim Sayyida Salme, if only

---

73 See E. van Donzel, pp. 63–70; see also page 23 in the *Addendum* above and G.S.P. Freeman-Grenville at pp. 329–30.
74 Citing Sir John Kirk's translation of her handwritten letter to Sultan Barghash in 1883, as provided in E. van Donzel, p. 53.
75 G.S.P. Freeman-Grenville at p. 308; see also *Memoirs*, p. 6.
76 From Colonel J.W.C. Kirk's summary of his father Sir John Kirk's files, appearing as an annex in G.S.P. Freeman-Grenville at p. 330. This is also corroborated in correspondence from Sayyida Salme's son Rudolph to his sister Antonie dated January 17, 1926, that was kept in the family of my second cousin, Alexander von Brand. This letter states that Barghash said the same to Sir Lloyd William Mathews, the English military leader (known as the "strongman of Zanzibar") during most of Barghash's reign, as recorded by Sir Rennell Rodd in 1893. Rudolph writes this in the context of his thoughts about potentially publishing his mother's writings.
77 As one of a series of policies enacted during this time, the *Gesetz über die Beurkundung des Personenstands und die Eheschliessung* marked an important shift from church-controlled marriages to state-controlled marriages that was largely aimed at the Catholic church, following the papal infallibility declaration as part of its *Pastor Aeternus* in 1870 and the rise of its *Zentrumspartei* (Center Party). Considering that this step towards marital freedom was decried at the time as an attack on religious freedom, it seems that not much in the playbook has changed 150 years later.

their timeline had been slightly delayed. But whether this emerging power struggle between church and state would have made a difference for them is unlikely. In their tightly wound, nineteenth-century society, this requisite civil marriage was still no substitute for church marriage.

Despite the progress in modern times, however, conversion from Islam is still seen to violate religious norms and remains controversial in some Muslim circles today. Even in Oman, the effort to balance tradition and modernity has reinforced some conservative strands. Religions are free to worship in certain areas, for example, but active proselytizing of Muslims is prohibited.[78] Despite Oman's showcased support of religious freedom that developed under Sultan Qaboos bin Said's reign (1970–2020),[79] residual concerns about someone like Sayyida Salme may linger. Over the years, I have wondered to what extent the Omani Sultanate would be ready to fully embrace a family member who is a great literary figure as the first Arab woman to publish a book,[80] and who is better known worldwide than any of her sibling Sultans, with arguably more name recognition than even her illustrious father—despite her conversion. Some may say that she received this visibility for all the wrong reasons, but I sense a different mood emerging. That many Omanis appreciate and love Sayyida Salme is something I feel unequivocally whenever someone from Oman finds out how I got my middle name.[81]

---

78 See the "2022 Report on International Religious Freedom: Oman" published by the United States Department of State through its Office of International Religious Freedom.
79 According to the Foreign Ministry of Oman's website on its Religious Freedom page: "Freedom of belief is guaranteed under the Basic Statute of the State. . . . The Omani Penal law stipulates that all the Abrahamic faiths (not just Islam) shall be protected from offence." www.fm.gov.om/about-oman/state/religious-freedom (2024) Oman also showcased its approach in a very successful traveling show that lasted a decade, from April 2010 through June 2019. Entitled "Tolerance, Understanding, Coexistence: Oman's Message of Islam," 125 exhibitions in 37 countries were sponsored by Oman's Ministry of Awqaf and Religious Affairs, under the project guidance of Mohammed Said Al-Mamari, now Minister since 2022, in collaboration with Arabia Felix Synform under Georg Popp. The 2019 status report notes that "[t]he success of this Omani-German venture demonstrates that constructive cooperation between East and West is, contrary to widespread opinion, quite possible even today . . . [as it] helps raise awareness and reduce misunderstandings about Islam, contributes to a public dialogue, and substantiates the positive image of the Sultanate of Oman." www.islam-in-oman.com
80 Others may assess to what extent the multiple Arabic translations of the *Memoiren*, both government-sponsored and privately published, have remained true to her original text, as opposed to leaving out religiously sensitive parts.
81 In case there is any question, no one in my branch of the family, from Rosa on downwards, has any current status within the royal family, nor, to my knowledge, has anyone in my branch actively sought reconciliation. This is in contrast to Rosa's brother Rudolph, who made it his mission to return to royal status. He was finally granted recognition in 1932 as a member of the royal family by Sultan Khalifa bin Harub, who reigned from 1911 to 1960. E. van Donzel, p. 125.

Holiday card fashioned after a stamp that was issued to commemorate the Sultanate of Zanzibar's independence (uhuru) from the United Kingdom, just a month before the Jamhuri 1964 revolution that deposed the Sultan

The situation seems much the same in Zanzibar. While conversion from Islam has some constitutional protections, it remains largely taboo and socially unacceptable. However, this is also a country that has a long history of religious tolerance, dating back to Sayyid Said's multicultural flourishing of society in the mid-nineteenth century that included active mosques, churches, and temples in Stone Town.[82] And far from disparaged, Sayyida Salme features heavily in the island's bid for tourists, notably these days with the Princess Salme Museum and Princess Salme Spice Tours. As far back as 1998 when my family first visited the island, Sayyida Salme even had her own room in the Palace Museum. Unfortunately, the building, which is the original Bet il Sahel described in the *Memoirs,* is now closed due to disrepair.

———•·———

When I step back, I am especially saddened to think it all stemmed from love. The conversion, the calumny, the casting out, the inner conflict—all because she expressed her physical, emotional, and spiritual self in her love for Heinrich and her love of God. How can such love be the root of such tragedy and agony? Precisely because she was true to her love—and that, I would suggest, was also rooted in her ability to love herself, to see her own value, to embrace her creative, inspired, and even boundary-breaking being. Later, it also reflected love for her children, when everything she did was ultimately for them. "It was only for the children that I sought to salvage whatever could still be salvaged. My own person was the least of my thoughts." (*Letters*, p. 89)

---

82 The influential and internationally respected Zanzibari historian, Professor Abdul Sheriff, penned an impassioned portrayal of this history in his essay titled "The Zanzibar Riots, the Union & Religious Tolerance" (2012).

In the raw repetition of her lived experience, the *Letters* keep returning to the question:

> Did I make the right choice in this regard? I must admit openly to you that I have asked myself this question so many times. Overall, I believe I handled the situation far too idealistically. . . . I did not approach things carefully enough back then, and instead gave exaggerated importance to ideals that I pursued with such effort and the greatest sacrifice. . . . The thought of continuing to live in this, for me, so incredibly complicated European setting, and the memory of my irreplaceable loss, often robbed me of my courage to go on. Above all, I was pursued by a constant feeling of abandonment that threatened to break my heart throughout every day. Under these circumstances, everything became so very difficult for me, and over time, I started to lose my resolve. "Strength, oh Lord, strength and steadfast perseverance!" remained my constant prayer for years. (*Letters*, pp. 72-73)

It was a constant prayer. And while her faith was rooted in her love of God, it was also rooted in her community. Her connection to God was in many ways how Sayyida Salme drew close to others, particularly in Zanzibar, where the beloved connections she had to give up were embedded in Muslim rituals. The memories recounted in the *Memoirs* feature the praying, fasting, major festivals, sacrificial offerings, marriage ceremonies, funeral rites, all described with deep attachment, all about her community. It was a matter of belonging. Being connected through Allah meant belonging to the tribe. As she described at the end of her second visit to Zanzibar in 1888:

> My siblings and relatives felt great compassion for me, and they beseeched me to become theirs again, to return to the old faith of my fathers and turn my back on the Germans. "Come, be ours again, for you belong to us! Do not go back to those strangers, but stay here with your family. We give you a sacred promise that you will have a good life with us." (*Addendum* at page 32 above)

This closeness, however, points to a disconnect. Sayyida Salme never writes about what it meant to abjure the faith of her parents, both of whom had been so devout. Surely, this also stung. It is not hard to wonder if she would/could have chosen Heinrich had her mother or father still been living, had it required a direct choice against them. But they were gone, her father having died in 1856 and her mother in 1859. Sayyida Salme, barely a teenager, says that she initially drifted "like a rudderless ship flailing about on a stormy sea" (*Memoirs*, p. 171). The ensuing post-coup rift in the extended family then intensified the sense of abandonment, leaving even more room for Sayyida Salme's community to shift. In the vacuum of her orphaned and shunned state, as her harem family pulled away, her chosen family became all the more important on this earth.[83]

And yet, her choice of Heinrich is another disconnect. Did she realize early on that he was not as full of faith as she? Soon enough, it seems, she came to understand that his connection to God was more superficial. For many in the secularized Hamburg where he was raised, Christianity was more of a social and cerebral experience, perhaps more head over heart, or as Sayyida Salme put it, more taught and less lived:

> It was always hard not to compare how little Muslims are taught about their own religion and yet exhibit such solid faith—in contrast to Christian children, who are so painstakingly instructed in school. I had the impression that religion is taught here more as mere science, to be forgotten again at the first opportunity or even oft-criticized, as I regrettably had to observe several times. (*Letters*, p. 65)

Although Sayyida Salme affectionately portrays Heinrich as a dear and devoted husband, and never disparages him in any way, in this area, she lacked his support. Not only did his devotion to God fall short of hers, but it also seems that he was unaware of the intensity of the gap, in part because she proved deferential to his nature and chose not to insist. She also seemed afraid to validate a difference that she knew was there, but preferred not to confront. I have wondered, if Heinrich had not died so soon, whether this fundamental asymmetry would have pulled at the harmonious balance between them over time. As it was, it proved one less dilemma she had to face.

After Sayyida Salme arrived in Germany, the whole context let her down and left her hanging. As important as faith was to her social fabric in Zanzibar, the initial lack of faith connection in Germany may have been a major reason for her separation from Hamburg society, including, it seems, the extended

---

83 One could say the same of her mother, Djilfidan, who was orphaned at age five or six, when Turkish mercenaries from Russian incursions raided her family farm, killed both parents, and rode off with her two siblings, never to be seen again. Sold into slavery, however, hers was not a chosen family. Even so, as a child and then *surie* in the harem, she found safety and solace. We do not know whether her original family was Christian or Muslim, although by the start of the 17th century, most Circassians had converted from Orthodox Christianity to Islam.

Ruete family.[84] This became more extreme after Heinrich died. She had no social currency without her husband, no cultural bridge to tide her over, and no active religious life to tie her in. Not until she met the Baroness von Tettau in Dresden, with whom she could finally learn and live her new religion, could she at last—seven years after arriving in Germany—speak of a meaningful Christian connection and a dearest, deepest faith friend once again.

> Through my new motherly friend, I was able to find the first true Christian, someone I had been seeking, unfortunately without success, all this time.... Oh, how often did my heavy heart lead me to her, since I could always be sure of her empathy and understanding. How often, oh how often, did I return home after being comforted and strengthened by her, able to continue the terribly difficult road in life. I could not thank the merciful Lord enough for his care. (*Letters*, pp. 84–85)

What was it about the Baroness that made such a difference? Even after Sayyida Salme moved to a new town, they kept close through correspondence. Von Tettau had originally sought her out, perhaps as a charity case, but they grew to appreciate each other in their mutual embrace of the Lord. Long after the Baroness passed away, Sayyida Salme kept her in heart and soul—never forgetting this crucial pillar at a crucial time. Indeed, mother figures played a prominent role in much of Sayyida Salme's life. Whether in the confines of the harem or the tumult of the West, Sayyida Salme thrived under the protective wings of older women around her—her mother, of course, but also her half-sister Chole, even as she led her astray, and the sisters Zeyane and ZemZem, in addition to the beloved Baroness who called her "my dear precious thing." I can see how they might have helped calm and guide Sayyida Salme's flapping wings.

What ultimately sustained Sayyida Salme, however, was how she communed with God. In the shifting spiritual terrain that underpinned her community on earth, God, it seems, was always with her. For all the breaches and brokenness, she was never alone.

And once she crossed over, she never crossed back. Sayyida Salme remained a Christian to the end of her days. It is meaningful that she never returned to

---

[84] It is hard to know whether this distance from the Ruetes stemmed from her or her husband's family. The record, including her writing, is noticeably silent on this score. Not even Ruete descendants I have spoken with were able to shed light on why there was so little apparent interaction between Sayyida Salme and her husband's extended family over the years.

On Faith

Islam, even after she gave up on Germany, even after her children had grown, even after she returned to Arab lands. There were surely many factors, not least her attachment to her children, whom she had deliberately and diligently raised as Christians. She felt tied to Christianity through them:

> I openly admit that I was often at the edge of my resolve, and naught but the thought of my children, who had been born and raised in the European way, kept me from succumbing to [the Zanzibari] pleas and staying with them in the beloved homeland. I valued the wellbeing of my children above my own happiness. Under no circumstances, not even for the most shining prospects, was I willing to sacrifice the emotional equilibrium of my children. (*Addendum* at page 33 above)

But perhaps she had also found peace with her Christian God. It is hard to know, but in a significant gesture, her son Rudolph sponsored an altar piece at the Protestant Church in Beirut in 1930 in memory of his mother.[85] When I think about it, though, one more thing may have been at play. At the deepest level, I can imagine that the painful memories of her conversion had so drastically seared her soul that the residual scars were simply too raw to be reopened. Despite all the cajoling of her Zanzibari fans—just come back, we promise you a happy life—she could not take it lightly. This, too, the all-encompassing gravity of her religious identity, was in the nature of her faith.[86]

As I reach the end of this essay, I can do no better than quote primarily from her. While I have relied mostly on the *Letters* to explore her conversion experience, it is the very last encounter in her *Memoirs* that makes me sit up and ponder the conundrum of it all:

> As I was approaching Zanzibar, I had been very unsure what reception would await me. That my brother would respect Germany's wishes, I had no doubt, and so it was. That he would hardly be kind towards me, at most putting on a good face in deference to Germany, for that I was also prepared. The ugly behavior he had shown my other siblings truly gave me no reason to expect any friendly outreach from him. But it was a different question as to how the population would react to

---

85 See correspondence with the *Evangelische Kirche* in Beirut at the Leiden University Libraries Or. 27.135 C9.
86 It seems fair to say that, as her views evolved, the border she crossed between religions proved more intractable than any border between nation-states. In her disappointment as a German citizen, she eventually saw the benefits of being a British citizen and second-guessed her own insistence on staying in Germany. (*Letters*, pp. 71–72) Her identity therefore did not appear to rest on her national status. Religion was the greater tie, the root cause of her trauma, even at a time when state and religion were so interdefined and intertwined.

> my sudden appearance. To my greatest joy, I can simply repeat that I received the warmest reception. Arabs, Hindus, Banyans, and natives, they all pressed me over and over again to please stay in Zanzibar. This fortified my belief anew that there was no way that religious hatred toward my person was at stake. . . . Such demonstrations of love and devotion have tided me over many a difficult hour, along with the blissful feeling of having seen my homeland once more. They have indeed made my trip a fount of delight for the rest of my life, and I can forever give thanks and praise to the Almighty for his goodness! (*Memoirs*, p. 227)

What a critical moment after all her hardship, what an important revelation this must have been for her! All the religious rules and social opprobrium that had taken so much from her were still no match for the human spirit. Two decades later, Sayyida Salme's enduring love of her homeland was reciprocated in the love of the people, who would not let religion stand in the way. What the church and the state condemned with their levers of hate still found refuge in the hearts of the local folk. Sayyida Salme's faith could transcend religion to find love and humanity. Her story is enough to give hope for today.

But look further at what I left out in the ellipses above, as it comes full circle:

> One day, I encountered two Arabs, with whom I began to converse. When another person pointed out that they were relatives of mine—I had not recognized them—I told them, if I had known, I would never have engaged in conversation, being so unsure about how my relatives stood towards me under the current circumstances. They immediately responded that, to them, I was still my father's daughter. And when I touched upon my religion, one of them countered that this had been predestined as my fate from the beginning of time. "Yes, the God that has separated you and us from the homeland is the same God that all people praise and adore; it is through his mighty will that you returned to us, and we rejoice in it. Is that not so? Will you and your children now stay here forever?" (*Memoirs*, p. 227)

History also records that even Sultan Madjid understood Sayyida Salme's behavior to be a manifestation of God's will.[87] Say what?! If her conversion and escape to Europe was in fact part of the Almighty's plan, how did she deserve to be so castigated and cast out?

---

87 Succinctly put by Sayyida Salme herself: "As a devout Muslim, he believed in divine predestination and was convinced that this alone had led me to Germany." (*Memoirs*, p. 202)

This, to me, is the strangest twist of all. Can it be that all the denigration, rejection, and danger, all her sacrifice, doubts and depression, inner conflict and pain, amounted to but a simple explanation that proved a complete excuse? True to Islamic principle, it was her fate. Her conversion was a betrayal, but it was also her destiny. That still implied a choice—that she could choose to revert—but it also anticipated the reverse. Today, if we are more sensitized to the balance of power, we can see that her original conversion was a form of coercion. But if even Islam, the religion that spurned her, answers that it was all foreordained anyhow, what was the offense of it all?

———•·———

I have written a number of essays for these books on key topics—on family, freedom, fear, controversy, inspiration, and more—but faith is the one I absolutely knew I had to write. And yet, I knew it would be the hardest to unpack. Faith is so profoundly present in her writings, and yet, for me, it felt too deep to reach, too sacred to touch. But now I have ventured forth nonetheless, in this centennial collection, and hope to have succeeded in my effort to illuminate, not obfuscate. I hope she would allow that I dared to tread so close. I hope she would approve of what I have had to say. It is now for you, those of you with faith and those of you without, to consider the meaning in it all and carry her touchstones to a throughline for today.

ON LEGACY

Sayyida Salme gave us her own legacy. It is one hundred years since she left this world and one hundred and eighty years since she entered it. In between, she lived a life that was remarkable in its contours, and all the more remarkable for what she wrote about it. Remarkable because she was the first Arab woman to publish a book, remarkable because she taught herself to write when it was taboo, and remarkable because so much of what she lived and recorded remains present and prescient for today. There is much to remark upon, and my various essays scattered throughout my three companion books[88]—including on family, fate, controversy, freedom, fear, inspiration, transits, faith, and now legacy—provide some of the cues and seek your reflections in return. The real legacy of Sayyida Salme lies in what we make of it.

That is how legacy works. We can leave behind as much as we want, but it has meaning only to the extent that those who come later pick it up. For this reason, I embrace the privilege and responsibility of sharing my great-great-grandmother's writings all these generations later in a worldwide language, a modern cadence, an attractive layout, and various formats (paperback, ebook, and audiobook), all to ease access to words that might make us ponder. Through her colorful, thoughtful, and soulful voice, we can allow some of the past into the present and aim for a better future.

We are all part of a continuum of time where the world that has been matters as much as where it is going. Anyone who has even a mild sense of history realizes that we are prone to revisit our foibles and failings again and again. Hard-won peace and prosperity become increasingly at risk the more time that passes since the last manmade calamity. We can feel it right now, and it becomes even more essential that we summon our better angels. Looking probingly into the past can remind us of what is at stake and where we went astray.

Sayyida Salme is just one life and one voice among multitudes to teach us. But it is in diversity that we can see most clearly. What other female voices do we have of the time, what other female Arab voices, what other female Arab Muslim-to-Christian voices? The value in paying attention to what Sayyida Salme wrote lies not only in her keen eye, witty spirit, bold assertions, and intimate

---

[88] The *Memoirs* (2022), the *Letters* (2023), and this *Centennial Collection* (2024), which are also available as a combined set in the *Centennial Compilation* (2024).

detail, but also in her convergence of perspective. Not only is her journey worth recounting, but it is the very source of her trenchant observations and penetrating insights—this overlay of Orient and Occident, this passage from Islam to Christianity, this descent from royalty to poverty. She lived a complex life that pitched external forces against internal fortitude. Her story gives us a prism to illuminate struggles we all face. In her self-expression, as she lived her life and as she wrote it down, she prods us to express ourselves.

And here, I am doing just that. In adding my voice to hers, I offer a stepping stone from her past that, in the words of my late brother, who deeply appreciated Sayyida Salme, may help us find our way forward:

> the stepping stones—
> which we skip *On*,
> crossing the universal pond
> make them part of the
>   going-from
> one thing
> to the next thing
> in our being
> and becoming[89]

---·•·---

Let history surprise you, let her story inspire you—
let her authentic voice speak to you.

---

[89] Martin Mathis Stumpf, August 15, 1963—August 18, 2005. Excerpt from a poem dated May 11, 2005.

In Memoriam

Emily Ruete,

born Sayyida Salme,

Princess of Oman and Zanzibar

* August 30, 1844
+ February 29, 1924

Sterbeurkunde.

Nr. 129.

Jena am 29. Februar 1924.

Vor dem unterzeichneten Standesbeamten erschien heute, der Persönlichkeit nach _____ bekannt,

der *Kaufmann Alfred Silling*

wohnhaft in Jena
und zeigte an, daß *Emily Ruete geborene Prinzessin von Zansibar*, der Verstorbenen wird auch als *Said bint Said* angegeben,
79 Jahre alt,
wohnhaft in Jena, *Gartenstraße 4*,
geboren zu *Zanzibar*, Witwer,

zu Jena in dessen Wohnung
am *neunundzwanzigsten* Februar
des Jahres tausend neunhundert *vierundzwanzig*
vor mittags um ____ Uhr
verstorben sei. Der Anzeigende erklärte, aus eigener Wissenschaft vom Sterbefall unterrichtet zu sein,

Vorgelesen, genehmigt und *unterschrieben*.
Alfred Silling.

Der Standesbeamte.
Oertel

Daß vorstehender Auszug mit dem Sterbe-Haupt-Register des Standesamts zu *Jena* _____ gleichlautend ist, wird hiermit bestätigt.

Jena am 1. März 19 24.

Der Standesbeamte.

Death Certificate, Nr. 129, Jena, February 29, 1924

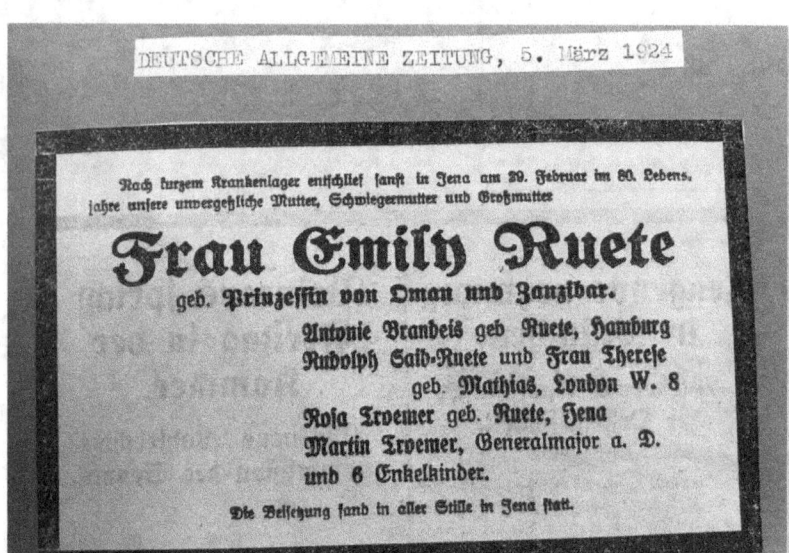

After a brief illness, our unforgettable mother, mother-in-law, and grandmother gently passed away in Jena on February 29, 1924, in her eightieth year.

Frau Emily Ruete
born Princess of Oman and Zanzibar

Antonie Brandeis, born Ruete, Hamburg
Rudolph Said-Ruete and Mrs. Therese,
born Mathias, London W8
Rosa Troemer, born Ruete, Jena
Martin Troemer, Retired Major General
and six grandchildren.

The private burial took place in Jena.

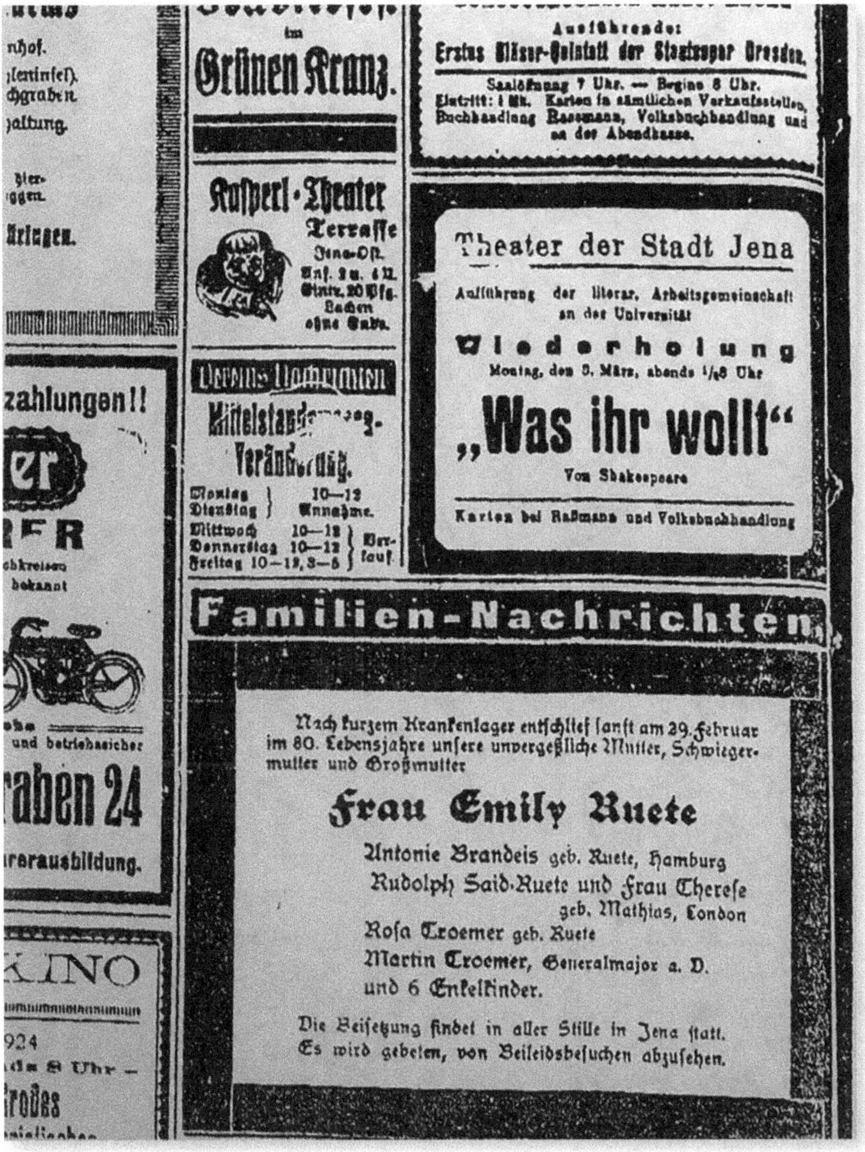

Sängerfest im Grünen Kranz.

Ausführende: Erstes Bläser-Solistat der Staatsoper Dresden.

Saalöffnung 7 Uhr. — Beginn 8 Uhr. Eintritt: 1 Mk. Karten in sämtlichen Verkaufsstellen, Buchhandlung Rassmann, Volksbuchhandlung und an der Abendkasse.

Kasperl-Theater Terrasse Jena-Ost. Anf. 3 u. 4 ½. Eintr. 20 Pfg. Lachen ohne Ende.

Theater der Stadt Jena

Aufführung der literar. Arbeitsgemeinschaft an der Universität

Wiederholung

Montag, den 3. März, abends ½8 Uhr

„Was ihr wollt"

Von Shakespeare

Karten bei Raßmann und Volksbuchhandlung

Vereins-Nachrichten

Mittelstands-...

Montag, Dienstag 10—12 Annahme. Mittwoch, Donnerstag 10—12, Freitag 10—12, 3—5 Verkauf.

...zahlungen!!

...graben 24

...rerausbildung.

KINO

...924

Familien-Nachrichten

Nach kurzem Krankenlager entschlief sanft am 29. Februar im 80. Lebensjahre unsere unvergeßliche Mutter, Schwiegermutter und Großmutter

Frau Emily Ruete

Antonie Brandeis geb. Ruete, Hamburg
Rudolph Said-Ruete und Frau Therese geb. Mathias, London
Rosa Troemer geb. Ruete
Martin Troemer, Generalmajor a. D.
und 6 Enkelkinder.

Die Beisetzung findet in aller Stille in Jena statt.
Es wird gebeten, von Beileidsbesuchen abzusehen.

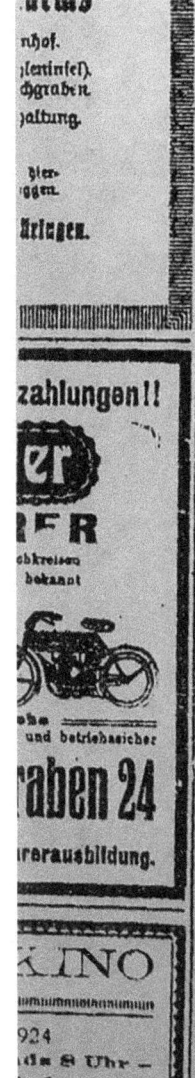

Sayyida Salme in 1908

Sayyida Salme in 1908

Sayyida Salme, back in Germany, in 1915

Sayyida Salme, in Berlin, in 1916

New Year's greeting card for 1922 with Sayyida Salme's face inserted

Signed photo from Rudolph gifted to Professor Christiaan Snouck Hurgronje in 1924

The family with Sayyida Salme's first grandchild from her daughter Antonie in 1901

The family with two grandchildren, from Rudolph (on lap) and Antonie in 1902

Some of Sayyida Salme's family with the Schröder family in Jena in 1919

Rosa's family at the baptism of her second grandchild in 1934

IV 18/25.

Abschrift

Beirut, den 14. Dezember 1910.

Mein letzter Wille.

Ich unterzeichnete Emily Ruete, geborene Prinzessin von Oman & Zanzibar, bestimme ich hierdurch wie folgt.

Nach meinem Ableben vermache ich hierdurch die Hälfte meines Vermögens bestehend aus Wertpapieren, welche in der Reichs-Hauptbank zu Berlin, teilweise auch bei der Centrale der Deutschen Bank zu Berlin niedergelegt sind, sowie auch mein gesamten Hausstand bestehend: aus Möbel, Silbersachen, Teppiche, Bücher, Kleidungsstücke, Wäsche, Bilder, Schmucksachen, sowie Alles, was ich im Hause besitze, meiner Tochter Rosalie Troemer, geborene Ruete.

2, Die verbleibende Hälfte meines Vermögens fällt zur Hälfte an meine Tochter Antonie Brandeis geb. Ruete &die andere Hälfte an meinen Sohn Rudolf Said-Ruete.

3, Tritt der Fall ein, dass meine Tochter Rosalie Troemer vor mir stirbt, so fällt das ihr von mir bestimmte Erbschaft vollinhaltlich nach Abschnitt 1 den Kindern zu, sie sollen Alles bekommen, was ich für ihre Mutter bestimmt habe.

4, Das Recht über die „Memorien einer arab. Prinzessin " sowie über die noch ungedrukte Manuscripte, meine europ. Leben beschreibend, soll meinen drei Kindern Antonie, Said & Rosalie & ihren Kindeskindern zu gleichen Teilen angehören.

Eigenhändig geschrieben.

Emily Ruete, geborene Prinzessin von Oman &Zanzibar.
Beirut, Syrien, den 14. Dezember 1910.

++++++++++

Initial Last Will and Testament from December 14, 1910, in Beirut

Transcription
Beirut, December 14, 1910.
My last will and testament.
I, the undersigned, Emily Ruete, born Princess of Oman and Zanzibar, set forth the following:
After my death, I hereby bequeath half of my estate, consisting of securities deposited in the National Bank main office in Berlin, in part also in the German Bank central office in Berlin, as well as my entire household consisting of furniture, silverware, rugs, books, clothing, linens, pictures, jewelry, as well as everything I own in the house, to my daughter Rosalie Troemer, born Ruete.
2. The remaining half of my estate shall go half to my daughter Antonie Brandeis, born Ruete, and half to my son Rudolph Said-Ruete.
3. In the event that my daughter Rosalie Troemer dies before me, then the inheritance set forth under point 1 shall go in full to the children; they shall receive everything that I have bestowed to their mother.
4. The rights to the "Memoiren einer arabischen Prinzessin," as well as the as-yet unpublished manuscripts that describe my European life, shall belong to my three children, Antonie, Said & Rosalie & their children in equal parts.
Written in the author's own hand.
Emily Ruete, born Princess of Oman and Zanzibar.
Beirut, Syria, December 14, 1910.

Last Will and Testament of Mrs. Emily Ruete, born Princess of Oman and Zanzibar.
In the year 1912, I drew up a will that was deposited in the local court of Spandau. Deviating from this will, I hereby set forth the following:
1. All my personal property, consisting of furniture, art, jewelry, linens, rugs, clothing, silverware, and the like, shall go to my two daughters, namely:
   (1) Mrs. Antonie Brandeis, born Ruete in Kl. Niendorf near Segeberg in Holstein.
   (2) Mrs. Rosalie Troemer, born Ruete in Jena.
   I wish for them to agree amicably on the division.
   As the only exception to this, I now order that my son, Mr. Rudolph Said-Ruete in Lucerne, be the one to receive all the items that come from Zanzibar.
2. My capital assets shall be divided equally among my three children, provided that if one of my children dies before me, such child's children shall stand in such child's stead.
3. In such event, my grandchildren shall not receive their shares before they reach the age of 25. Naturally, the children may already have use of the assets before reaching the age of 25. Until the age of 25, the administration of this estate shall reside in the hands of:
   (1) Mr. Rudolph Said-Ruete, or if he has died,
   (2) My son-in-law General Troemer, or if he has died,
   (3) My daughters, in order of age.
4. I name my son Said-Ruete as executor of my will, in the first instance, or if he should die, my son-in-law, General Troemer.
Jena, September 30, 1920.
Emily Ruete, born Princess of Oman and Zanzibar.

Final Last Will and Testament from September 30, 1920, in Jena

Translated on page 93 above

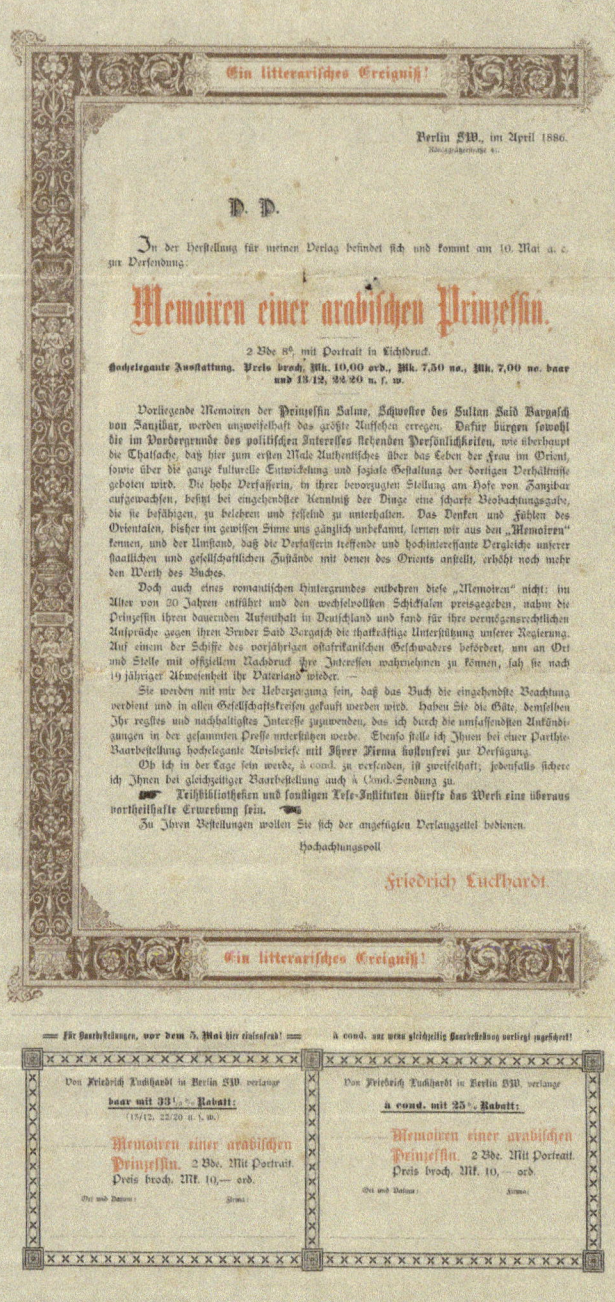

A literary event!

Among the publications for my publishing house, the following will be available for distribution on May 10 of this year [1886]:

Memoirs of an Arabian Princess

----

2 Vols., 8°, with a collotype portrait.

Very elegant arrangement. Regular price per book 10 Marks, ordered in advance 7.50 Marks, ordered in advance and paid in cash 7 Marks; and 13/12, 22/20, and so on.

The present Memoirs of Princess Salme, sister of Sultan Said [sic][90] Barghash of Zanzibar, will without a doubt evoke the greatest interest. This is assured not only by the prominence of politically important individuals, but also the general fact that authentic details about the lives of Oriental women, as well as the overall cultural development and social organization of local conditions, are presented for the first time. The distinguished author, who grew up in a privileged position in the royal court of Zanzibar, possesses a deep knowledge and a talent for keen observation that enable her to instruct you and keep you captivated. In the "Memoirs," we learn about the thoughts and feelings of Orientals, heretofore in certain ways completely unknown to us. That the author additionally provides fitting and fascinating comparisons between our national and social conditions and those of the Orient further heightens the value of this book.

These "Memoirs" are also not lacking in romantic content. Having eloped at the age of 20 and subjected to the most turbulent fortunes, the Princess took up permanent residence in Germany and received vigorous support from our government for her inheritance claims against her brother Said Barghash. Traveling on one of the ships of last year's African squadron, which allowed her to pursue her interests with official pressure, she saw her homeland again for the first time in nineteen years.

You will share my conviction that this book deserves the most avid attention and will be purchased by all levels of society. Kindly give it your most energized and sustained interest, which I will support through widely distributed announcements to the entire press. In addition, if you undertake a partial-cash order, I will offer you very elegant publication notices with your company name at no extra cost.

Whether I will be in a position to send books à condition is unlikely; in any case, I ensure you à condition shipment for a simultaneous cash order.

This would be an exceptionally advantageous acquisition for borrowing libraries and other reading institutions.

Please use the order form provided below for your purchases.

Respectfully,

Friedrich Luckhardt

A literary event!

---

90 See footnote 31 above.

In the press: "she is described by all who meet her not only as energetic, but also highly-educated/cultured"

Translation of a paragraph which was published in the
"MOKATTAM" of Thursday 27th 1924 No.10771

DEATH OF AN ARABIAN PRINCESS.

News from Berlin announced these days the death of Mrs. Emily Ruete a Princess of Zanzibar of the Barghash dynasty, sister of Sultan Saïd late Sultan of Zanzibar. She was eighty years of age when she died. This is the history of this Princess: She met a German merchant of Zanzibar, she loved him, she did her best to talk to him and succedded. He married her and took her back to his country from fear of her relatives. He had from her one boy and two girls and he died very young. Some time after, the boy entered the service of the German Army and the writer of these lines made his acquaintance and that of his family when he was Military Attaché to the German Consulate General at Beyrouth. After that he became Manager of the German Oriental Bank at Cairo. His name is Said Ruete. This name, Said, was the name of the Sultan his uncle. [grandfather]

The Princess, Mrs.Ruete was well acquainted with the Arabic language and was able to speak it gramatically and always with a loud and clear voice in a way that surprised all those who heard her for the first time speaking arabic when wearing a european dress and hat. She was a farsighted and very intelligent lady. The daughters inherited the intelligence of their mother and one of them is well acquainted with Arabic, German, English, French and Italian and learnéd by heart in ènglish the famous verses of Homer's Iliad and Milton's poem "PARADISE LOST" also in English and both are the longest poems known up to our time; she is also clever in music and singing.

The Sultans of Zanzibar come originally from Yemen and still have some relations with Hadramaut.

Cairo-based Al Muqattam article translation sent from the British consulate

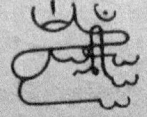

To the Memory

of my Mother

the

SEYYIDAH SALME

(*Emily Ruete*)

Daughter of **SAID BIN SULTAN**

who

born at Zanzibar on August 30th, 1844, and having fulfilled a great mission by a life that proved to the West the noble qualities of the Womanhood of the East,

died at Jena on February 29th, 1924.

Rudolph's dedication to his mother in the biography of his grandfather

Ivy leaf from the Ohlsdorf gravesite placed in Sayyida Salme's copy of the Memoirs

The cremated remains of Emily Ruete, born Sayyida Salme, were buried next to Heinrich Ruete, her husband, in the family plot at the Ohlsdorf Cemetery in Hamburg on June 14, 1924. The plot consists of multiple gravesites located at U27, Nos. 78–89.

From a letter by Antonie to her brother Rudolph on June 15, 1924:

> Many thanks for your letter from the 6th of this month. The burial of our mother's urn took place yesterday. Several days earlier, [we] had brought a palm tree, as you had requested.... I laid out the black cloth in the stone container, then came the soldered Memoirs, followed by the metal covering, and on top of that the sand from Zanzibar. After the cemetery official was satisfied that everything was done according to the regulations, and the name on the metal covering was consistent with the formal submission, the Witte employee cemented the stone lid shut and cemented [on] the number that was recorded in the cemetery register. Cornelius Jacobs then said some very beautiful words about the life and character of our mother, which touched all our hearts. The official then shoveled dirt onto the stone container and placed upon it the pretty wreaths that relatives and [others] had brought....

From a letter by Rosa to her brother Rudolph on June 15, 1924:

> ... We placed the ashes, the soldered Memoirs and the sand from Zanzibar in the cement container that already lay in the ground, which was then walled shut (after inspection by the official) ... Toni and I had already gone there the day before and had a deep impression of this solemn space, a wonderful spot on the forest floor. I gave special thanks to Uncle Hermann that Mama could find such a lovely resting place; we would have had nothing comparable to offer. Now she lies there, in such a peaceful place, with the appeasing and calming effect of nature's presence in this beautiful time of year. We had placed benches at the location and stayed for a while....

The Ruete family gravesite at Ohlsdorf Cemetery in Hamburg, Germany

Map of the Ruete family's gravesite at the Ohlsdorf Cemetery in Hamburg

Emily Ruete
Widow of Rudolph Heinrich Ruete

born August 30, 1844, in Zanzibar,
died February 29, 1924, in Jena.

Whosoever loves his homeland as you do,
is loyal to the core.

SALAM

It might be odd to close this book with a "hello"—salam to all who have perused these pages! But in the typical richness of Arabic, this ubiquitous little word goes both deep and wide.[91] It has within it a promise of peace and protection, no aggression, no offense, no evil. It signals safety, allowing surrender and submission. Its root appears in Islam, meaning submission to God, and salamah, meaning peace and security. In As-Salam, it is one of God's ninety-nine names. In the phrase Dar As Salam, it is paradise.

Salam is also the root of Salme, the name Djilfidan gave her second daughter, after the first one died very young.[92] What hopes this mother would have had for her child, that it might survive and thrive! In Djilfidan's status as a *surie*,[93] this precious newborn was a gift to the Sultan, a step-up in status as the mother of royalty, and a pass to freedom upon the Sultan's death—but also, naturally, far more than that. After Djilfidan's early loss of father, mother, sister, and brother, with no other direct family known to her, this little girl had a special status. I would like to think she completed Djilfidan's world and made her whole in a way that nothing else could. I can imagine that Djilfidan chose the name Salme for all its deeply comforting and connecting meanings, grateful to have found such comfort and connection for herself, within a larger family and toward God, and wishing all the same for her beloved child. I do believe this chosen name reflects a wish for the wholeness of self we all seek.

---
91 It also goes far, as a greeting and word for peace, safety, and well-being in Swahili as well.
92 *Memoirs*, p. 7. Note that this detail was left out of both historical English translations, the ones from 1888 and 1907. See my comments at www.sayyidasalme.com/translation.
93 Plural *sarari*. This refers to the "secondary wife" type of concubine in the Omani harem. (*Memoirs*, p. 249)

Sayyida Salme's writings tell us how well *that* went—even to the point of effacing her name. But throughout all the transitions, despite all the hardship, she maintained a remarkably strong core of confidence and steady connection to her maker.

Although she became Emily Ruete, I still refer to her as Salme in recognition of her deepest self, that inner strength at the root of her salam. As she speaks to us today, she is still Sayyida Salme to me, and I will trace my own roots to her mother in recognition of my own mother. My mother and I are two steps in this cascading history, and with her, I have had the privilege of this shared endeavor. For all three books in this series, I am ever so grateful for my mother's gracious and generous support, her careful review, insightful contributions, unending stamina, and complete devotion to the project. This has been a wonderfully grounding and fulfilling collaboration, very much in the spirit of salam.

And with that, I can now also say ma'a salama to say good-bye—in the greater sense of the proverbial "God be with you"—with wishes of goodness and wholeness for all.

LIST OF IMAGES

[Front cover] See [85] and [89] below.

[7] Lithograph of the British sailing ship *HMS Highflyer*, said to be from 1861, artist unknown. This twenty-one gun, corvette class warship of the Royal Navy was launched in 1852 and participated in the 1854 Crimean War on the Black Sea and then the Second Opium War, before transitioning to African shores in the mid-1860s. It appears that the *Highflyer* was patrolling the waters around Zanzibar for illegal slave trade and rescued 152 slaves from an Arabian ship in August 1866, just days before Sayyida Salme came on board to be taken to Aden, Yemen. One of them was a young African boy, who eventually took the name Thomas Malcolm Sabine Highflyer after the Royal Navy captain of the ship, Thomas Malcolm Sabine Pasley. This boy worked on the ship for two years before he was adopted by a family in Brighton, but then died in 1870 from tuberculosis and dropsy. "New grave for freed slave Thomas Highflyer who lived in Brighton," by Jack Arscott, January 21, 2018, *The Argus*. Young Thomas may well have been on the ship with Sayyida Salme. The *Highflyer* completed its sailing days in August 1868. www.pdavis.nl under Royal Navy Vessels.

[9] Photograph and notes about Captain Thomas Malcolm Sabine Pasley, a British Navy captain who picked up Sayyida Salme from the open water on a late August night in 1866, first heading south and then north to Aden, thus enabling her secret departure from her homeland. The clippings were pasted by Sayyida Salme's son Rudolph into a book that is part of the collection he provided to the Oriental Institute, namely R.N. Lyne, *Zanzibar in contemporary times: a short history of the southern east in the nineteenth century* (1905), at the Leiden University Libraries in the Said-Ruete Collection under SR423.

[10] Studio portrait of Sayyida Salme taken by photographer H.F. Plate in Hamburg around 1868, not long after her arrival in Germany, and used as the frontispiece for her 1886 publication of *Memoiren einer arabischen Prinzessin*. From the translator's family collection.

[11] Cover page of a compilation of Sayyida Salme's legacy writings prepared as typed manuscripts by the family after Sayyida Salme's death in 1924 and formally presented as her *Literarischer Nachlass* (Literary Estate) to various institutions by Sayyida Salme's son Rudolph. This compilation includes the two

texts that are translated in this collection: *Nachtrag zu den Memoiren* (see "Addendum to My Memoirs") and *Syrische Sitten und Gebräuche* (see "Syrian Customs and Conventions"), in addition to *Briefe nach der Heimat* (published in a separate companion book as "Letters to the Homeland"). The *Literarischer Nachlass* is located in the Leiden University Libraries at Or. 6281.

[12] One of six of Sayyida Salme's half-brothers that reigned over Zanzibar as the Sultan, following their father's death in 1856. Sayyid Khalifa bin Said became Sultan in 1888, when Sultan Barghash died, and continued until his own death in February 1890. A mounted engraving can be found in the Leiden University Libraries at Or. 27.135 D28.

[15] Top: Note to the Oosters Instituut (Oriental Institute) included in correspondence related to the Institute's acquisition of books and materials donated by Rudolph Said-Ruete; located in the Leiden University Libraries at Or. 127.35 J1. Bottom: The bookcase made to house the donated collection.

[16–17] Original pages of the *Nachtrag zu den Memoiren*, appearing in a single notebook, handwritten by Sayyida Salme, with edits from her son Rudolph and daughter Rosa; in the Leiden University Libraries at Or. 27.135 A1.

[18–19] Revised pages of the *Nachtrag zu den Memoiren*, appearing in a single notebook, handwritten by the author's daughter Rosa, with edits from her brother Rudolph; in the Leiden University Libraries at Or. 27.135 A2.

[20] First page of an early typewritten copy of Sayyida Salme's *Nachtrag zu den Memoiren*; provided by Alexander von Brand from his family collection.

[21] First page of an upgraded typewritten copy of Sayyida Salme's *Nachtrag zu den Memoiren* that is part of the compilation described under [11] above; from the Leiden University Libraries at Or. 6281.

[23] This handwritten copy of the original Arabic poem received by Sayyida Salme after her second departure from Zanzibar in 1885 was produced by her daughter, Rosa. The author of the poem was a half-sister from the harem, but her exact identity is not known. Rosa's brother, Rudolph, pasted Rosa's copy into a family edition of the *Memoiren*, with the notation that it was "copied from the original by Rosa Troemer-Ruete; Jena, October 1924," half a year after Sayyida Salme's death. It was also marked with two corrections by the family friend, Professor Christiaan Snouck Hurgronje. This copy of the *Memoiren* is located in the Leiden University Libraries at SR 614b.

[30] The two-masted *SS Neckar*, with screw propulsion at a service speed of fourteen knots. It sailed for the Norddeutscher Lloyd shipping line from 1874 to 1895, first transatlantic and then in the Far East service as of 1886. www.ggarchives/oceantravel/immigrantships. Image credit to the Peabody Museum of Salem (the Peabody Essex Museum).

[35] Watercolor and drawing from the "Album von Zanzibar von William O'Swald & Co." O'Swald is likely the competitor company that Sayyida Salme referred to disparagingly in the *Letters* (p. 66). These are two of more than thirty photographs and paintings in the album, which was compiled in 1899 to commemorate fifty years of the company's presence in Zanzibar. Image credit to the Northwestern University Libraries through their digital collection at www.dc.library.northwestern.edu.

[41] Photograph of Rosalie Ruete, known as Rosa, the translator's great-grandmother. She was Sayyida Salme's youngest and a mere four months old when her father tragically died. From what we know, Rosa was particularly close to her mother, including as the only child that accompanied her on the second trip to Zanzibar in 1888. Her even script is also particularly visible in marked copies of her mother's writings on which they collaborated. Rosa was gifted in languages and studied art with Max Rabe. At age 32, on September 17, 1902, she married Captain Martin Gottlob Reinhold Troemer, who later became Major, then Major General. She had two daughters, Emily (1903) and Berta (1904), both of whom received PhDs (in law and chemistry, respectively), which was unusual for women at the time. Rosa took care of her mother, first in Bromberg and then Jena, from the time her mother left Beirut in 1914 until she passed away in 1924. Rosa died in Kronberg(Taunus) in 1948. Much appreciation to Ursula Luther, a descendant of Heinrich Ruete's sister Sarah (née Ruete) Rothenbücher, for sharing this image from her private collection.

[42–43] Pages from the original *Syrische Sitten und Gebräuche*, appearing in a single, mostly empty notebook, handwritten by Sayyida Salme, with a cover entitled "Beirut;" in the Leiden University Libraries at Or. 27.135 A6.

[44] First page of an early typewritten copy of Sayyida Salme's *Syrische Sitten und Gebräuche*; provided by Alexander von Brand from his family collection.

[45] First page of an upgraded typewritten copy of Sayyida Salme's *Syrische Sitten und Gebräuche* that is part of the compilation described under [11] above; from the Leiden University Libraries at Or. 6281.

List of Images

[50] Photograph of the first wedding of Sayyida Salme's children, when her eldest, Antonie, married Eugen Brandeis in Beirut in 1898; generously provided by Alexander von Brand, a descendant of Antonie, from his private family collection. Shown is the celebration at the Hotel Bassoul, with the bride and groom in the center. Sayyida Salme is standing behind the groom and Rosa is left of Antonie. Antonie was 30 at the time, and Eugen Brandeis was 22 years her senior in his second marriage. Immediately after the wedding, the couple moved to Jaluit in the Marshall Islands, where he served as the imperial governor of the German protectorate from 1898 to 1906. Antonie gave birth to two daughters (Margarethe in 1900 and Johanna in 1904). The couple divorced in 1913. A detailed account of Antonie's remarkable work as one of very few female ethnographers at the time and her support of German colonialism appears in the thoroughly-researched final project report from Godwin Kornes for the Museum Natur und Mensch in Freiburg titled "Provenienzforschung Ozeaniensammlung Eugen und Antonie Brandeis (Ethnologische Sammlung)" (2022). See also his brief essay titled "The Ambivalence of Gender" at boasblogs.org (2022). Godwin Kornes contacted us in connection with this research. I am immensely grateful to him for his support of my work on Sayyida Salme and our family's reconnection through him to Antonie's branch of the family through her great-grandson Alexander von Brand.

[51] Top: Photograph of one of Sayyida Salme's later residences in Beirut starting in 1909, as part of a series of photographs included in an album compiled by her son Rudolph and included in the materials he gave to the Oriental Institute in Leiden in 1937; located in the Leiden University Libraries at Or. 27.135 H5. Bottom: Photograph of the same house from the same series; also at Or. 27.135 H5. Rudolph added the red x's to mark his mother.

[52–53] Two photographs of the interior of Sayyida Salme's home in Beirut from an album of photographs that was included in Rudolph Said-Ruete's collection of books and materials he granted to the Oriental Institute in Leiden; the album now resides in the Leiden University Libraries at Or. 27.135 H5.

[57] Certification of Sayyida Salme's baptism under the "Christian Name Emily" on May 30, 1867, as an extract from the official Register of Baptisms at Aden, Yemen, signed by the "Chaplain for Aden." More than a name change, this act constituted her conversion from Islam to Christianity that sealed her self-exile. It immediately preceded her wedding vows to Heinrich Ruete in the same church on the same day. The form incorrectly notes her age as 30; she was still 22. The certificate is included in Rudolph's collection in the Leiden University Libraries at Or. 27.135 C4.

[64] Rudolph Heinrich Ruete's signed oath of citizenship for the independent city of Hamburg (*Freie und Hansestadt Hamburg*) dated April 17, 1868. Born in Hamburg of German parents, Heinrich had been a German citizen all his life, including during his decade as a German merchant based in Zanzibar—until he married Sayyida Salme. Unbeknownst to him at the time, this foreign marriage was considered an act of disloyalty. Heinrich's effort to reinstate his citizenship status proved relatively minor, but quite significant, not least because it paved the way for his wife to acquire Hamburg and German citizenship even after his death. Leiden University Libraries at Or. 27.135 C4.

[65] Certification of Emily Ruete's status, in her position of widow, as a citizen of the State of Hamburg and thus also the newly-constituted German Reich dated May 1, 1872. Unlike her husband's citizenship declaration above, no oath of loyalty or signature was required. The only signature appearing here is of the relevant agent of the issuing Hamburg police authority. Leiden University Libraries at Or. 27.135 C4.

[69] Holiday greeting card to the Stumpf family from Said El-Gheithy, received in the early 2000s. We first got to know Said El-Gheithy in connection with his 2001 exhibit "Princess Salme—Behind the Veil: The Life and Writings of Sayyida Salme, Writer and Teacher (1844–1924)" at the Brunei Gallery of the SOAS University of London and maintained some contact with him thereafter. From the Stumpf family's private collection.

[81] Death certificate of Emily Ruete, who died of double pneumonia on February 29, 1924, at the age of 79 in the home of her daughter Rosa at Gartenstrasse 4, Jena, in eastern Germany. Not long after World War II, Rosa left the house in Jena when she received permission to move from the Russian zone to the American zone to join her two daughters in Kronberg (Taunus) near Frankfurt. This permission was granted on the basis of an attestation of support from Friedrich Oechsner, who was then living in Washington, DC, with his wife Olga. Olga Salme (née Said-Ruete) was Rudolph's daughter and thus Rosa's niece. The family's copy of the death certificate is in the Leiden University Libraries at Or. 27.135 C4.

[82] Death notice pasted into an album prepared by Sayyida Salme's son Rudolph and titled "Zum Tode von Emily Ruete" (Relating to the Death of Emily Ruete). Located in the Leiden University Libraries at Or. 27.135 C2.

[83] Death notice published in a local newspaper under the header "Family News" along with other notices of the day for theater, opera, and cinema

performances. Much appreciation to my uncle Helmuth Schwinge, a great-grandson of Sayyida Salme, who provided this copy.

[84] Framed studio photograph of Sayyida Salme, undated and unattributed, but presumably from the same 1908 studio session as [85]; the framed portrait stands in the Schwinge home and was photographed by my cousin Emily Schwinge.

[85] Framed studio photograph of Sayyida Salme dated December 1908, according to a handwritten notation ("XII/1908") on the same photograph in the Leiden University Libraries at Or. 27.135 D7; the framed portrait was provided by Alexander von Brand from his family collection.

[86] Studio photograph of Sayyida Salme taken by Progress-Photographie, with handwritten date of February 1, 1915, a year after Sayyida Salme returned to Germany, on the framing cardstock that is somewhat damaged by liquid below; provided by Alexander von Brand from his family collection.

[87] Studio photograph of Sayyida Salme taken by A. Wertheim in Berlin, with a handwritten date of 1916 on the back along with a notation in Arabic that reads "many greetings" (*salam kathir*); located in the Leiden University Libraries at Or. 27.135 D6.

[88] Handmade holiday card wishing a happy new year for 1922, with a figurine cut-out body in a fur coat and a face of Sayyida Salme pasted in from an actual photograph. For some blog-inspired thoughts, see my short piece 101 years later at www.sayyidasalme.com/post/prosit-neujahr. The card is part of Rudolph's collection in the Leiden University Libraries at Or. 27.135 D8.

[89] The same studio photograph as in [85] above, in this case accompanied by a photograph of Sayyida Salme's son Rudolph and his handwritten dedication dated October 1924 to Professor Christiaan Snouck Hurgronje ("Herrn Professor Dr. C. Snouck Hurgronje das Bild meiner ihm in aufrichtiger Wertschätzung verbunden gewesenen Mutter, Frau Emily Ruete/Prinzessin von Oman und Zanzibar, freundschaftlichst zugeeignet—RSaidRuete"), apparently presented as a gift following her death; from the Leiden University Libraries at Or. 27.135 D7.

[90] Top: Studio photograph taken by E. Bieber on December 8, 1901. Shown from left to right: Rudolph Said-Ruete and his British Jewish wife Theresa (née Mond); Sayyida Salme; Antonie Brandeis (née Ruete); Antonie's young daughter Margarethe; and Rosa Troemer (née Ruete); provided by Alexander von Brand from his family collection.

[90] Bottom: Studio photograph taken by W. Höffert on September 15, 1902. Back from left to right: Rudolph Said-Ruete; Rosa (née Ruete) Troemer; Rosa's husband, General Martin Troemer; Antonie (née Ruete) Brandeis, and Antonie's husband, Eugen Brandeis. Front from left to right: Theresa (née Mond) Said-Ruete; Rudolph's young son Werner; Sayyida Salme; and Antonie's young daughter Margarethe. Provided by Alexander von Brand from his family collection.

[91] Top: Photograph taken in Jena at Beethovenstrasse 15 on June 22, 1919, of Sayyida Salme's family with the Schröder family, close friends that she first met in Beirut, with a continued friendship back in Germany. Paul Schröder was the same age as Sayyida Salme and served as German consul (1882–1885) and then consul general (1888–1909) in Beirut during the time Sayyida Salme lived there. The names on the cardstock were written in by a member of the Schröder family and are noted here in italics. Back from left: *Herr Troemer* (Martin Troemer), *Mama* (Lucie Schröder), *Frau Ruete* (Sayyida Salme), *Lukki* (a Schröder daughter), and *Frau Troemer* (Rosa Troemer). Front from left: unclear (possibly another Schröder daughter, although probably not Hedwig "Hedi"), *Emily Troemer* (the translator's grandmother), *Otto* (a Schröder son), and *Berta Troemer* (another Troemer daughter).

[91] Bottom: Adding the next generation beyond Sayyida Salme in a photograph taken at the baptism of Rosa's second grandchild, with the following handwritten notation on the back: In remembrance of the baptism of Renate Schwinge in Halle on April 22, 1934. Back from left: Berta (née Troemer) Prausnitzer, and two unknown gentlemen. Front from left: Martin Troemer, infant Renate Schwinge, Emily (née Troemer) Schwinge, Emily's husband Erich Schwinge, and Rosa Troemer. From the translator's family collection.

[92] First last will and testament from Emily Ruete recorded in Beirut, Syria, on December 14, 1910, with a date notation at the top left of April 18, 1925 (perhaps the date it was typed up), with a handwritten notation "Abschrift" (transcription) at the top center (perhaps to denote the carbon copy of an original typed page). This will is part of the family collection in the Leiden University Libraries at Or. 27.135 C6(1), but was superseded by later wills, the last of which is also part of the collection (see next item).

[94–95] Third and final last will and testament from Emily Ruete recorded in Jena, Germany, on September 30, 1920. This will refers to a second will from 1912, which is missing from the family collection, but may conceivably still be preserved in the referenced *Amtsgericht* of Spandau. This final will resides in the Leiden University Libraries at Or. 27.135 C6(2).

[96] Printed flyer by publisher Friedrich Luckhardt in Berlin announcing the upcoming publication of Sayyida Salme's *Memoiren einer arabischen Prinzessin* in 1886. To great acclaim, a total of four editions of the *Memoiren* were published that same year. The flyer is in the Leiden University Libraries at Or. 27.135 A7.

[98] Two published drawings that appear amidst dozens of clippings from newspapers and periodicals that were placed in a scrapbook kept by Sayyida Salme's son Rudolph. Top: This drawing appears above an article titled "Sister of the Sultan from Zanzibar" with the handwritten note "Illustrierte-Zeitung—1884," presumably referring to the popular weekly *Illustrirte Zeitung* (1843–1944). Bottom: This drawing appears alongside a response to a question from a reader in Milan with the handwritten note "Schorers Familienblatt [Schorers Family Paper] No. 31. 1886." Located in the Leiden University Libraries at Or. 27.135 C1.

[99] Translation of an extract titled "Death of an Arabian Princess" from the Mokattam newspaper on March or April 27, 1924, conveyed to Rudolph Said-Ruete from someone in the British Consulate in Cairo by letter dated May 12, 1924. The copy includes some fine pencil markings correcting the text. Located in the Leiden University Libraries at Or. 27.135 C3.

[100] Dedication at the front of Rudolph Said-Ruete's biography of his grandfather, Sayyid Said bin Sultan, who governed Oman and Zanzibar from 1806 to 1856. Rudolph Said-Ruete, *Said bin Sultan (1791–1856)—Ruler of Oman and Zanzibar: His Place in the History of Arabia and East Africa* (1929).

[101] Ivy leaf from the Ruete family's gravesite at the Ohlsdorf Cemetery in Hamburg that was taped into Sayyida Salme's copy of the *Memoiren*, with a handwritten notation likely from her son Rudolph dated May 1931. Sayyida Salme's own signature in Arabic appears at the top left. This is the same copy of the *Memoiren* that contains the handwritten Arabic poem described in [23–25] above. Part of the Said-Ruete special collection of the Leiden University Libraries at SR 614a.

[103] From the Ruete family gravesite at the Ohlsdorf Cemetery in Hamburg. Photograph taken in October 2020 and generously provided by Godwin Kornes. The name Emily Ruete is one of several etched into the *Erinnerungsspirale* in the *Garten der Frauen* at the Ohlsdorf Cemetery. She is also included in R. Bake and B. Reimers, *Stadt der toten Frauen: Frauenportraits und Lebensbilder vom Friedhof Hamburg Ohlsdorf*, pp. 205–8 (1997).

[104] Two photographs taken almost a century apart of the Ruete family gravesite at the Ohlsdorf Cemetery in Hamburg. Top: Mounted and undated photograph in the family collection; located in the Leiden University Libraries at Or. 127.35 D14. Note the palm tree planted between the headstones of Heinrich and Emily Ruete that was added at Rudolph's request per a letter to him from his sister Antonie on June 15, 2024 at Or. 127.35 C4(6). Bottom: Photograph taken in October 2020 and provided by Godwin Kornes.

[105] Schematic of the Ruete family gravesite prepared by the translator.

[106–7] Three photographs from October 2020 by Godwin Kornes.

[108] Photograph from August 2023 of the translator and her mother, Andrea and Ursula Stumpf, working on the *Letters* translation, with a thank you to the translator's sister, Silva Stumpf, for spotting us.

[118] Photomontage presented by Rudolph to the Zanzibar Museum in 1927; much appreciation to Torrence Royer, curator of www.zanzibarhistory.com.

[Back cover] Top: See [10]. Bottom: Sayyida Salme's signature on the left, see [101]; on the right, as printed on the title page of her published *Memoiren*.

www.ingramcontent.com/pod-product-compliance
Lightning Source LLC
Chambersburg PA
CBHW050225100526
44585CB00017BA/2018